T

7

TITANIA'S NUMBER

7

Titania Hardie

CONNECTIONS
BOOK PUBLISHING

For my father, father-in-law, mother-in-law, stepson and sister!

A CONNECTIONS EDITION
This edition published in Great Britain in 2007 by
Connections Book Publishing Limited
St Chad's House, 148 King's Cross Road, London WC1X 9DH
www.connections-publishing.com

Contents

STARTING THE JOURNEY

This little book of numerology invites you to be amazed by what you will learn from numbers — about your character, your tastes, your instincts, your relationships, and even about your future. But to do this involves a willingness to believe — as Pythagoras, the 'Father of Numbers' did — that numbers can provide a clue, or formula, through which we can perceive some of the evolving patterns and cycles that affect our own individual existence.

Let's find out more ...

Discovering numerology

Fans of Sudoku will understand how it entices us intellectually to see how strands of numbers – almost magically – slot together and interconnect with one another, revealing a rhythm of harmonious relationships between the lines. In one sense, numerology does this for us on a personal and spiritual level. The Science of Numbers, as it is called, suggests that there is an order and a rhythm in the universe of which we are a part, and although there is a certain mystery in the way numbers seem to function as symbols for our experiences, there is a long tradition across many cultures of their fascination for us.

Now, in an age of gigabytes, PINs and mathematic-based technology, how can we doubt the role that numbers play, or the way in which they have become part of our daily landscape? Numbers speak to us every day about

6 5 4 3 2 1 9 8 7

our personal identity on this planet. Our birth date is absorbed by society as proof of our existence: you need it to be 'real' at the bank, in the office, when you travel, in an automated phone queue – in *all* official records. Indeed, many people consider the day-date of their birthday to be their lucky number. But can it really say anything about us?

Did you know, for instance, that:

- If you were a **5** or a **9**, you'd need to invest in good-quality luggage because you'd be bound to notch up a lot of air miles?
- Or that a **4** will painstakingly spend hours getting something just right, whereas a **1** will rush in and get several projects started, full of enthusiasm, only to leave someone else to carry them through to completion?
- And a **3** is a born entertainer, who enjoys spending time with others, whereas a **2** prefers to live quietly,

with just one or two partnerships, both socially and in business?

But you've picked *this* little volume because you're a **7**, which means that you're choosy about company and guard your privacy more than any other number – a perfectionist who is critical of everyone, but most of all yourself. A **6**, on the other hand, would be more easy-going, while an **8** would work frantically, and then take a crowd out to lunch on their bill!

About this book

Each individual title in this series investigates, in depth, the meaning of one of nine personal numbers. *This* volume is dedicated to the exploration of the number **7**.

We will be focusing principally on your **DAY** number – that is, the number relating to the day of the month on which you were born (in your case, the 7th, 16th or 25th of the month). Calculating your **DAY** number is easy: you simply add the digits of your day together (where applicable), and keep adding them until they reduce to a single number (*see calculation examples on page 270*). And that's it. It doesn't matter which month or year you were born in – you just need the day-date to discover your **DAY** number. And *you're* a **7**.

Your **DAY** number reveals all kinds of information, and, working from this number, we will be considering:

- The obvious attributes of your number as they impact on your personality
- How you are likely to dress, and what colours or styles appeal
- How you react to things psychologically, and what drives or motivates you
- What annoys you most

7   8   9   1   2   3   4   5   6

- In which fields you will have the most natural abilities and gifts
- What sort of lover you are, and how you relate to all other numbers
- What the future holds

... and much, much more.

And you have another significant number too: your **LIFE** number. This is derived from adding up the digits in the *whole* of your birth date – day, month and year *(see examples on page 270)*. What does *this* number mean, and what do your **DAY** and **LIFE** numbers mean in tandem? And how does it affect you if you're also a 'master' number (**11** or **22**)? Read on and you'll see. But first, let's meet your **DAY** number ...

6   5   4   3   2   1   9   8   7

So, you're a 7

7

Both **philosopher** and **dreamer**, you are a serious thinker with considerable **intellectual gifts** and a **drive** to do the best you can in this lifetime. In one sense, your fate is dictated entirely through your own mind. What you imagine and research, learn and analyse, will influence the people you become involved with and the places you visit – both imaginatively and actually. You are attracted by some of the **mystical** elements of life, wondering what is real and what is myth, but always holding a strong conviction that there is more to know.

7 as a number is often quite **serene** and reflective, but this may disguise a mind that is in ceaseless turmoil, full of **contemplation**, going over important situations time and again. Your number is the most meditative, fascinated by

7   8   9   1   2   3   4   5   6

what makes people tick, usually having a strong political conscience but also being critical of shallowness in people or social values. You are **highly intuitive** and often quite unconventional in your appraisal of others; yet you will *never* suffer fools – gladly or at all! This can make you very **demanding** – but also fascinating – in a love bond.

A **student of life** and relationships, you learn from the circumstances you are thrust into. Life throws some testing situations your way, but after the initial jolt which knocks your spirits flat, you will use these challenges to plumb the depths of life's inner meaning. This gives you a tremendous **resilience in adversity** – though it may not be clear that you are in control for the first hour of a crisis. Given time and **quietude** – quintessential for a 7 – you will turn every drama into a defining experience. You may write or lecture about it, or simply weave it into the work you do; but somehow all others benefit from the **wisdom** and **spiritual growth** of a 7; it is your mission, and anything less would be a travesty. You may **never feel satisfied**, though, for it is **7**'s lot to feel that there is always room for improvement, for greater knowledge, for more understanding.

Your number is not frivolous or extravagant, and although you love things of **quality** with a high aesthetic appeal, you are never worried about the commercial value of an idea or object. In fact, **7** is likely to challenge accepted norms here, being critical of what society thinks is important or desirable. **7**s don't always make their lives simple, and are **rarely happy with second best**.

If a **7** falls below their own standard of achievement, they can become deeply **depressed** and lonely, retreating into their shell, **over-analysing** what has gone wrong, demanding too much from partners and family, finding it difficult to ask for what they want. This is partly because there is a hidden force at work, to look behind the material aspects of life and go into a special realm of dream and thought. Poetry and literature may become vital in the life

7   8   9   1   2   3   4   5   6

of a **7** — more so than countless friends. Music, too, fulfils a vital need for lifting a **7**'s spirits and heightening their feeling and **intuition**.

Because **7**s so often seem to leave behind the mortal desires of this world, you may be seen by some as a **loner**. **7**s do indeed remain single quite often, or form relationships with others that allow a huge amount of **private time** and space. **7** needs this isolation, but it can be confusing for loved ones who feel they are not wanted or that they have caused offence. An understanding partner will recognize the need for **independence** without becoming paranoid.

The push towards **perfection** makes **7**s specialists at whatever they do, but they are **highly critical** and should put this characteristic to good use without being intentionally cruel! You have a fine nose and a good ear, an eye for things often lost on others, and a brilliant memory for words. You are, in fact, altogether **refined and dignified**, but if you become maudlin through lack of achievement or a feeling that you haven't created anything to be proud of, you may be far **too hard on yourself**. It's hard to rescue a **7** who feels they have let themselves down, and problems like drinking too much, or becoming too isolated, may cause difficulties. A negative **7** is a gloomy soul who can become reclusive, whereas a positive **7** is an **inspirational force** with the capacity to lift others out of despair in their crisis hour.

Sound familiar? Getting a taste for what your number is about? And this is just the beginning. You'll soon find out how the number 7 expresses itself as your Day number in each and every day of your life. But before we go any further, let's take a look at where all this first came from . . .

| 7 | 8 | 9 | 1 | 2 | 3 | 4 | 5 | 6 |

What's in a number?

Numbers have always had a sacred meaning. The Egyptians used an alphabet that conflated letters and numbers, and, as such, each number exuded an idea that was more than the sum it stood for. There is a whole book of the Old Testament devoted to the subject; and the Hebrew language – exactly like the Egyptian – has a magical subtext of meaning where letters and numbers can be doubled to reveal an extra layer of secret, so-called 'occult' information. It is called the *gematria*, and forms a crucial part of the sacred occult wisdom called Kabbalah. There were twenty-two letters – a master number – in both the Greek (Phoenician) and Hebrew alphabets, and repetitions of the spiritual properties of the numbers **3** and, especially, **7** recur throughout the Bible.

6 5 4 3 2 1 9 8 7

The Father of Numbers

But modern numerology derives more formally from Pythagoras, the Father of Numbers, who was a serious and spiritual philosopher, as well as the man who explained some of the secrets of geometry. Born on the island of Samos, although he ultimately settled in Cretona, a Greek colony in southern Italy, he is understood to have travelled widely to both Egypt and Judea. Some accounts of his life also suggest he may have studied under the Persian sages of Zoroaster, but an analysis of his teachings certainly reveals the strong influence of Kabbalistic thought in his philosophy.

Pythagoras understood numbers as a *quality* of being, as well as a *quantity* of material value. In one sense, the numbers as figures were connected with the measuring of things, but 'number' itself was significantly different to this, and encompassed a spiritual value. The numbers from one through to nine represented universal principles through which everything evolves, symbolizing even the stages an idea passes through before it becomes a reality. Mathematics was the tool through which we could apprehend the Creation, the universe, and ourselves. Musical harmony was a sacred part of this knowledge, as was geometry, which revealed divine proportion.

Most importantly, Pythagoras believed that numbers were expressive of the principles of all real existence – that numbers themselves embodied the principles of our dawning awareness, our conjecture and growth. Through mathematics and number we could approach divine wisdom and the workings of the universe as a macrocosm. Thus, in microcosm, our personal 'mathematics' would unlock the workings of our own being, and help us to see a divine wisdom concerning ourselves. **1** was not just the first digit, but also had a character of beginning, of independence, of leadership, just as the number **2** was more than merely the second number quantifying two objects, but also implied the philosophical concept of a pair, of co-operation, of a relationship beyond the individual.

Pythagoras also believed that we could understand our direction and fate through an awareness of repeating cycles of number, making numerology a key to revealing our opportunities and our destiny.

By tradition, the doctrine Pythagoras taught to his students in the sixth century BCE was secret, and no one wrote down his ideas until his death. But Plato was a follower of Pythagoras and, along with the rebirth of Platonism, the ideas of the Father of Mathematics were revealed afresh during the revival of Greek learning in the Renaissance. The great magi of the fifteenth and sixteenth centuries explored anew the significance of number and the gematria, to understand the hidden messages of the ancients and of the divine mind. Mathematics as a philos-ophy was the bridge to higher realms of spirituality.

| 7 | 8 | 9 | 1 | 2 | 3 | 4 | 5 | 6 |

Essence of the numbers

one is the spark, the beginning, Alpha, the Ego of consciousness. It is male.

two is consort. Adding partnership, receptivity, it is female, bringing tact.

three is a synthesizing of both of these qualities and brings expansion and joy.

four is the number of the Earth, of the garden, and of stability. It brings order.

five is curiosity and experiment, freedom, changes. It brings sensuality.

six nurtures and cares for others. It will love and beautify, and brings counsel.

seven perfects and contemplates the Creation. It is intellect, stillness, spirit.

eight is the number of power, the octave, a higher incarnation. It brings judgement.

nine is humanity, selflessness, often impersonal and all-knowing. It brings compassion.

6 5 4 3 2 1 9 8 7

Applying the knowledge

A deeper understanding of the self can be achieved through an awareness of the mysticism of number within us; and both the birth date and, to some degree, our given name are the keys to unlocking our mystical, spiritual core of being. Exploring the affinity between letter and number can also reveal insights about the lessons we need to learn throughout our lives to improve and develop as individuals (*see page* 25).

This book looks at the significance of numbers as they affect us every day, focusing largely, as introduced earlier, on our **DAY** number. It is this number that reveals to us our instincts, our impulses, our natural tastes and undiluted responses, our talents and immediate inclinations. This is how people see us in daily situations, and how we behave by essence.

We will be exploring how our **DAY** number influences

7   8   9   1   2   3   4   5   6

our love relationships and friendships; at what it says about our career strengths and our childhood; at the way our number manifests in our leisure time; and at how it might give us a better understanding of what to expect in our future cycles, as we pass through any given year under the sway of a particular number. Each birthday initiates a new cycle, and each cycle seems uncannily connected with the philosophical concerns of the number which governs that year. Look both to the past and present to see how strongly the number-cycle can illuminate our experiences ... and then count ahead to ponder what may be in store over the next year or two.

And numbers also say something about where we live or work, about our car, and even about our pets. Understanding these secret qualities can add a new dimension of pleasure — not to mention surprise — to our journey through life.

6　　5　　4　　3　　2　　1　　9　　8　　7

A NUMBER TO GROW INTO

The presence of our **LIFE** number, however, takes longer for us to appreciate in ourselves – longer for us to grow into – and it often takes time to reveal itself. This number comes to the fore as your life progresses, and on pages 214–247 we will be looking at the meaning of your **DAY** number together with your individual **LIFE** number, to see what this reveals about your character and potentiality.

The **LIFE** number may intensify the experience of the **DAY** number – if it is closely related to it, or shares similar patterns. But more frequently our two different numbers clash a little, and this often allows insight into the aspects of our being where instinct pulls us in one direction but higher wisdom or experience mediates and pulls us in a second direction.

Who would have thought you could learn so much from a number? Pythagoras certainly did, over 2,500 years ago ... and now you will discover it too.

7   8   9   1   2   3   4   5   6

What's in a name?

Your name also has a story to tell, and it is a story revealed through number. Every letter corresponds to a number: in the Western alphabet we use twenty-six letters, which are at variance with the twenty-two formerly enshrined in the Hebrew and Greek alphabets. Some numerologists believe that this is in keeping with the more material world we now live in, as the number '26' reduces to '8' (when you add the digits), which is the number of power and money.

The correspondences between the numbers and the letters of the alphabet are as follows:

1	2	3	4	5	6	7	8	9
A	B	C	D	E	F	G	H	I
J	K	L	M	N	O	P	Q	R
S	T	U	V	W	X	Y	Z	

6	5	4	3	2	1	9	8	7

As you are a **7**, it is most revealing to look at the letters G, P and Y as they occur (or not!) in your name. This is because they intensify the experience and impression of your main number.

To make the most of the qualities inherent in your number, you should be using a name which is in poetic harmony with your **DAY** number. As a **7**, you feel the need to perfect, and you will also be at your sharpest intellectually if you have a name which underlines these bright **7** qualities. Using a name which includes a G, P or Y bolsters your powers. If this sounds strange, consider that many of us have our names shortened or played upon by friends, family and lovers, so it is important to feel that our chosen name – the one that we use as we go about in the world – is making the best of our abilities and energies.

Among the letters that are equivalent to the number **7**, Y can be a vowel or a consonant – so the chances are that you have this letter in your name or nickname. It is especially significant if your name starts with a '7' letter, or if the first 'vowel' in your name is a Y, because this strengthens the power of your number **7** at the beginning of your name. Create a nickname or pet name with it in, if necessary, just to back up the outstanding properties of thought and precision that come with your number.

The letter-numbers help us to act out our sense of purpose, and if these work in correspondence with the DAY number we are more likely to find our sense of will and achieve our goals more rapidly. But if we have few, or none, of the letters of our DAY number, we often feel it is much harder to shine in our field of opportunity.

Missing a '7' letter?

As a **7**, you rely on philosophical ideas about the world and your feelings for others, but if you have no '7' letters in your name you may need to develop your mind and

6   5   4   3   2   1   9   8   7

independence more, and listen to your intuition about people and events. You may be bright but lazy, or you may crave truth and yet feel deceived by others often.

Don't allow the material world, or your material needs, to offset your ideals and goals. Find a way to work a '**7**' letter into your life – as a company name or pet name, for instance, or by altering the spelling of your name. Then you will gain confidence about your abilities and ties with others.

Too many 'G's or 'P's?

It can be just as much of a problem if your name carries a flood of letters which correspond to your number. Too many 'G's could make you resent advice given from others; and you may be difficult to persuade. A dominant P, or several 'P's, makes you clever and clear-sighted, but also potentially selfish. Y as the first letter, or with several

7	8	9	1	2	3	4	5	6

in your name, confronts you with choices at regular intervals, and probably means you hate restraint.

A dominant cluster of these letters – say, a first letter of one name, and a surname emphasizing another – bestows robust health and, indeed, an interest in health generally. But too many may make you too much of a lone spirit! Try to choose a name for everyday use that strikes a good balance.

YOUR DAY NUMBER
It's a new day ...

You will learn a lot about the numbers of your birthday and your name as this book unfolds, but the DAY number is, to my mind, the most important – and sometimes least well-recognized – number of all ... the number which exerts a magnetic hold on us each and every day of our lives. Every time we react to a situation, an emotion, a provocation of any kind, we are shooting straight from the hip, as it were, and this reaction is coloured by our DAY number.

7   8   9   1   2   3   4   5   6

As we know, your 'Day Force', or **DAY**, number is **7** if you were born on the 7th, 16th or 25th of any month. Each of these different dates also affects us – the characteristics of the number derived from a birthday on the 16th vary intriguingly from one on the 25th, for instance – and we will look at these differences in the pages ahead.

All three dates, however, still reconcile to an overall **7**. This number determines your gut reactions and the way you express yourself when you are being most true to yourself. Your parents, lovers, friends and co-workers all know you best through this number.

So what is the theme of being a 7? What are you like when you're at work, rest and play? And how compatible are you with the other numbers? Let's find out …

6 5 4 3 2 1 9 8 7

7'S CHARACTER
Charms, graces, warts and all ...

With a natural hauteur and demeanour that makes others wish they had such effortless panache, yours is a number that oozes style and nobility. No one confronting you on any level – whether personal or in business – will ever try to bluff you, or put in less than an honest contribution, more than once. 7s soon become known as people not to be messed with – someone who will eat idiots or freeloaders for breakfast! You know at a glance whether a person has something important to offer, and, as long as you're impressed with their candour and willingness to do something properly, you will have an interesting collection of peers, friends and business associates.

A 7 is only ever impressed with real substance.

| 7 | 8 | 9 | 1 | 2 | 3 | 4 | 5 | 6 |

Soul purpose

Your number is concerned with the soul of things: of people, and of the earth. You are in quest of what has not yet been understood, and those you choose to do this research with will be those whose intentions are pure and who have a good soul. This is not always recognized, and others are sometimes inclined to think you're a snob. But **7** can't help its natural superiority – and, if you are a snob, it is likely that you are an intelligent and well-informed one! Someone's lack of class or breeding is not at issue: but if anyone has a paltry soul, or a mean nature, or a dis-inclination to understand the wider picture, they will never become close to you.

Although the number **7** is repeated so often in the Bible, it is not purely a religious number: in fact, you may not be conventionally religious at all. It is, however, a *holy* number — seeking something holy in the nature of the universe and the potential of humankind. This frequently makes **7**s a law unto themselves, with a personal creed that is stronger than anything learned. Your habits, for instance, may border on compulsive tendencies, and you may be irritated by anyone else who is unclean, or ill-informed, or who eats unhealthy food. This is because **7** wants to look to the best that we can all be as individuals. Sloppy work is not an option, nor is half-prepared information. And yet you are a wonderful host, and will give much time to others who like to be around you — as long as they are birds of a feather whose interests and mind appeal to you.

Fair's fair

Life for a **7** is not always easy, as you are articulate and a deeper thinker, and so find it impossible to stay silent regarding anything you feel is unjust. A **7** will go out on a limb for anyone in their family who is denied or harshly dealt with; and the **7** parent of a child who is bullied is a force to be reckoned with. If there is any odious bureaucracy in the world in which you function, you're certain to take it on with gusto. A **7** boss, for example, would willingly be dismissed on behalf of an employee; or, if anything or anyone has been evaluated inequably, **7** sets out like Sir Galahad, to redress the wrong. **7** has the powers of speech of an angel and the mind of a clear-thinking scientist: beware anyone who takes you on without knowing this!

Despite a fine mind and an enigmatic, impressive personal stature, 7s are shy and sometimes lacking in confidence. This is because you are constantly urging yourself on, towards greater achievement and deeper knowledge. A **7** will never waste time or words. Even though this is the number of pithy wit and rhetoric, **7** embodies the idea that less is more, and that speech is silver but silence is golden. Everyone else is often left wondering what a **7** really thinks!

Even if you happen to be one of the more outspoken and ambitious holders of your number, you will also be prudent and diplomatic. You feel strongly that you should be fair in your dealings with others, and if anything puts you in a situation where this is of counter-interest, such as a company policy handed down to you from above, you will feel very unhappy, and may even become ill over it. Being seen to be fair is a code of honour for you, and you will often find that your business relationships are especially strong because of the reputation you have built up for fairness.

Hidden connections

With an inclination towards close observation and reading below the subtext, 7s never take anything at face value. It is a particular gift of this number that it can see the connection between situations and facts which are lost to

> **Keynotes of the 7 personality**
>
> **Positive associations:** wonderful powers of observation and analysis, sophisticated taste, natural sense of dignity and integrity, charming disposition, deep thinker with good rational mind, intuitive, spiritual
>
> **Negative associations:** may be argumentative and hyper-critical, sometimes arrogant, not always able to be freely generous, can be cynical or emotionally repressed, demands too much of self and others

most people, and your capacity to relate people and events is sometimes uncanny. This is a huge benefit in business — although 7s are rarely driven to simply make money for the joy of it; but if you are interested in what you are doing, and find a rationale behind it, you are able to put your sharp, analytical mind to brilliant use, especially as you partner it with astute intuition.

6   5   4   3   2   1   9   8   7

Your personal style is distinctive, marked by the aristocratic aura you exude. 7 is refined and has a particular sensibility, which makes it unlikely that anyone will ever hear you speak coarsely. It is almost impossible for you to lose your poise and apparent serenity, but if you become too wrapped up in material goals or personal dramas you may forget that you have this glowing quality and descend into gloom and despair. Yours is not a number that often asks for help, giving one and all the impression of self-sufficiency and – indeed – superiority. Who would dream of offering advice to the wisest of people? And yet, talking things over with an intelligent, gentle soul would help to remind you you are not alone!

Natural escape

Taking trips to the woods or the sea are vital for your survival sometimes, for 7 draws from nature more than any

7 8 9 1 2 3 4 5 6

other number. Coming face to face with the wild can be bracing but also provide a comfortable platform for your philosophical and spiritual self. Sometimes this is all it takes to fathom out a problem, so it is important to prioritize such quiet time spent pondering eternity. This doesn't make you any less modern, or an unhappy urban dweller (**7** is usually more at home with a high-tech kitchen and a string of galleries and museums to visit), but the escape – the permission to withdraw and find some secret place – is actually crucial to your well-being.

When you set out into the world, you always prefer to be clean and well-groomed. **7** is just not a sloppy number, and what it regards as 'weekend wear' would pass for 'chic style' in anyone else's language. Generally, **7**'s taste in clothes dictates that you avoid bold patterns in bright colours, favouring simple classics that are well-cut. You may feel most comfortable in pastel colours or neutrals, and natural fabrics like linen and silk and cashmere feel at home next to your skin. Your taste is excellent – if anything, quite understated – and your hair is likely to be frequently shampooed and stylishly cut. Anyone will know if you are unhappy or emotionally stressed, for it is only then that you become less attentive to your personal style – a certain telltale sign that something is wrong.

Serene creativity

Deep in your soul you may feel introspective and reserved, but you often dazzle the world with your verbal brilliance and flair for the unexpected. Even when you are prepared to go out and be 'on show', your natural inclination is for peace and a healthy environment. In a certain mood of laconic thinking and philosophical musing, a **7** might be comfortable getting 'lost' in a noisy, smoky bar; but it is more common to find you being intolerant of others' loudness or brashness, and happier in your own company

7	8	9	1	2	3	4	5	6

– or with selective friends – in a more serene and clean environment. Indeed, it can be awkward for those living with you to accommodate your needs in this regard.

A wise **7** will always be able to ensure their domestic harmony by finding a handy path to a beach near to where they live, or perhaps a footpath through the woods. That solitude required for introspection is not an idle need: you must have calm to develop your ideas and think creatively, and this need is stronger in you even than in someone born with the number **1**.

Your creativity is specialized, and you don't like dabbling in anything: a **7** must learn all that can be learned about their area of specialization. You have a good head for solving difficulties in other people's businesses, and your creative mind can find a niche market or untapped reservoir of interest, and provide exactly the right product for that market. Normally you are also quite wise about money, and you will rarely be a spendthrift.

Spiritual leanings

I have not as yet said much about your spirituality, but **7** is indeed a mystical number that seeks a higher wisdom, even if by choice you have elected to be agnostic or atheist. Your natural rhythm of reflection and meditation reminds us that **7** is the forefront number in the Bible, used more than three hundred times in both Testaments. The Bible tells us it is the number sacred to God.

Regardless of your religious beliefs, **7** finds a way to express this mysticism – even through the medium of science or research. Yet many **7**s will choose to investigate a range of spiritual philosophies – from learning yoga to an interest in Masonic ideas. Your special depth of character has a religious aura, and, with or without a conventional faith, you are an excellent teacher of ethics and a spiritual seeker.

| 7 | 8 | 9 | 1 | 2 | 3 | 4 | 5 | 6 |

Spelling test

We looked earlier at the importance of the letters in your name, and how the name you use can help you to underline your strengths of discernment and intellectual focus. The letter G helps you stand firm in moral arguments, and a name with a predominant G will probably also deepen the mysticism in your character: yet, you may be sceptical of many things, and be hard to persuade on any number of issues. The letter P underlines the creative talents of the number **7**, and if your name contains a prominent P you should be particularly talented in specialized creativity – anything from painting to cooking. Y deepens **7**'s love of beauty and also adds a strong affinity to touch: you may well enjoy sculpting or potting, and, unlike **6**, you don't mind getting your hands dirty in the cause of perfection – as long as you can wash them afterwards and rub in some hand cream!

6 5 4 3 2 1 9 8 7

Any of the three '**7**' letters will help you express your intuition and also underline your musical ear and your good taste and nose. If you lack them you may find that you're always unsure of your abilities, or that you feel unable to live up to your own dream of what you should be. **7** needs to feel pride in its achievements, and without a '**7**' letter in your name you may feel that such personal pride evades you a little.

Seeking sanctuary

Many people see you as an enigma – difficult to know well, hard to understand; or they may not 'get' your sense of humour or your take on the world. But you care little for others' opinions of your philosophy. You know that, in troubled times, *you* are the one they seek: go to a **6** when you need a cuddle, but a **7** is the one with the good mind.

With a poetic heart and a secretive side to your dreams

and wishes, you will never settle for second best. And often this means that **7**s have a bold sense of what the future can be. But when things get too much for you – when you find your inspiration drying up – it is time for a retreat, either alone or with a like-minded thinker who will give you breathing space. The need to recharge your mind and your energies is constant, because of the very high level at which you function, and it will be germane to keep this in mind when you are closely involved in a love relationship. Only having some 'space' will keep things alive.

When **7**s love, they do so with great intensity, but don't be surprised if there are periods in your life when you are alone again. It may be that this is the way your relationship functions – that one of you will travel while the other has private time. Or it may be that relationships cannot keep pace with you, and you find that you must live alone again for a time. Don't panic or fight this: **7** must have such a space and such a calm to perform at the best

level. Time for reflection and personal stock-taking will
be thrown at you repeatedly, but it does not have to be
indicative of the whole of your life. When relationships do
become problematic, it may be that you are being asked
what is really important to you; and you may have to
allow someone in – which can be harder than you think!

Get the balance right

In a life that will be exceptional and complex, you must be
prepared to see the importance of your soul as the gov-
erning force in your life. For **7s**, the soul must direct the
body with powerful help from the mind: but – astute as
yours is – the mind is not enough. **7** is looking for the soul
of the human race and of the world. This places a starry
canopy of possibility above you: what you do within that
universal scope is up to you. Unselfishness can be your
greatest personal characteristic, and, equally, criticism of self

7　8　9　1　2　3　4　5　6

and others can topple your best intentions. Getting these gifts in balance will be the task of your life. I am not a **7**, yet of all the numbers, **7** is that which I respect the most.

7 in a nutshell

Personality watchwords: shrewd, discriminating, dignified
Lucky colours: old-fashioned rose/burgundy, brick red, carmine pink
Lucky herbs/flowers: bay, parsley, basil, whortleberry, lily, lupin, hollyhock
Scents: green tea, frankincense, sandalwood, verbena
Fashion style: clean colour, refined fabric, simple cut with classy tailoring
Decorative style: open space, white, garden brought into home, antique or modern, not fussy or over-decorated
Letters: G, P or Y (needed in the name you use)
Car style: practical but dignified – can go anywhere!
Holiday destination: old civilizations with places to explore – Paris and Greece favourites

Which 7 are you?

3   4   5   6   **7**   8   9   1   2

Everyone with a **DAY** number of **7** will exhibit many of the characteristics just discussed. It is interesting to see, though, how the number **7** varies across all of its incarnations. There is a subtle but definite difference between the way the number operates for someone born on the 7th of the month – which makes for a pure **7** effect – and someone born, say, on the 25th.

As a rule, anyone born on the single-digit date has the truest and most undiluted effect from the number, whereas someone born as a product of two digits borrows some qualities from the pairing of the numbers. Twenty-anything puts the softening digit '2' before the second number, and this usually means that, whatever number you are, you are more aware of the needs of others. Similarly, if '1' is the first digit (16th) you are more independent, and perhaps more assured of your ability, than other **7** people (but possibly a little more selfish, too).

*Let's look at the variations across all
the birthdays . . .*

| 6 | 5 | 4 | 3 | 2 | 1 | 9 | 8 | 7 |

Born on the 7th?

Everything in your life depends on being in the right state of mind. More than any other **7** you must have quiet reflective time, and you need to weave in habits that allow you thinking space in every single day — whether that means travelling alone to work or walking the dog before the day has begun. Five minutes in the shower is not enough! Quality is your standard in everything, and only by giving yourself breathing/creative space can you deliberate on what it is in your pursuits that will help you attain that quality.

All people born under number **7** reach out for a greater understanding of life, and work to achieve intuitive insight with others; but this birthday makes you even more conscious of the desire to know and learn more about *why* we are, and to delve into the mystery of the world. This, too, compels you to withdraw from the hustle and bustle of daily living, and it would be astonishing to find someone with this number content to be in the city only. A pure **7** must have an escape in the country – either with family or friends, or regular excursions into green space, in lieu of a permanent rural base – although the sea also offers an excellent retreat.

Your taste is subtle, and you understand what makes perfection in others as well as yourself. This forces you to strive for perfect achievement in whatever business you pursue, forging new degrees of brilliance. You are prepared to learn and research more to make a project or career duty the best that it can be. You will probably only choose to work with those who inspire and stimulate you, learning from them in the course of your work, too.

Your desire to understand yourself is paramount, and sometimes means you are criticized by those who think you self-indulgent and prone to 'navel-gazing'. You are ultimately determined to think for yourself at all costs, and this, too, can mean you run the gauntlet of popular opinion. It is simply that the push to find intellectual clarity and an awareness of life's purpose is the shaping theme in your mindset. Remember, though, that this can make you unreasonable with others sometimes: things that make sense in your reflective mind may have little reference to the way others think and feel outside your own realm of experience.

It may be a feature of your life that you have many unusual and extraordinary experiences as a result of time spent alone. Sometimes conditions arise over which you seem to have little control, and everything is subtly moving you into these situations to prompt you to think and meditate. 7s are choosy, and often seem to be forced to go it alone; but this is part of the plan for the development of your distilled state of mind, and it is easier if you go with it when such conditions occur. Fighting against the rhythms of your life will make everything more complex and tortuous. Try to look behind the reasons why some events come up for you, often in repeating cycles.

If pain and difficulty come at moments in your life — as they must for us all — your mental response lays a foundation for your inner strength. You have the capacity to make huge changes in your life as a result of insight, and new goals and plans loom in your new consciousness after each small setback. With such a fine mind it is essential you pursue your education, and that you learn to distinguish between what is fascinating possibility and what is pure gullibility: cultivating your sense of *reason* is crucial as a partner to your *intuition*.

Like all **7**s, your nose should be excellent and your palate sensitive. **7**s have a cultivated reaction to perfumes, and can never be haphazard in their choice of what they like. A pure **7** birthday also makes you an excellent cook of healthy food, and you'll enjoy cooking for select company.

6   5   4   3   2   1   9   8   7

Born on the 16th?

This is a fascinating birthday, held by real achievers and thinkers. '16' is regarded as a 'karmic' number, with the implication that you have been here before and that your inner sense of experience is deeper and more expansive than your years in this world *now* seem to allow. '16' is said to carry difficult experience from a previous time with all the wisdom and depth of fellow-feeling that this brings with it. Thus it is not the easiest birthday, and yet it belongs to many who have a richer, more profound experience of life. Nothing will be handed to you on a plate; but you may leave the rest of us staring in astonishment at what you make of your life. '16's are defiant, self-motivated and smart, and more strongly compelled than anyone else to strive, attain and be something in this life.

In the tarot, '16' is the card known as 'The Tower',

7   8   9   1   2   3   4   5   6

which has been struck by lightning; and this proves a good image to shed light on the number. Frequently required to react to sudden events, you have the inner power to build your life from the ruins of the past. Others will be amazed at the courage you show over and again in facing down serious obstacles. And yet, after a time of pain, your path to joy is clearer, and your ability to rise out of the ashes of adversity is extraordinary. Things won't be smooth, but those born on this day are made of strong stuff and have exceptional gifts – and are almost certain to use them!

If this all sounds like too much to process, it should be said that anyone with this birthday has a special personal magnetism. Your strong character attracts many people to you, and your specialized talent is above the norm. With a gift for music, writing, painting or dance, as well as academic study and scientific thought, you stand out in the crowd. You may feel that your personal empathy for suffering would make you a good politician – and this is a

6   5   4   3   2   1   9   8   7

possibility. You are very emotional and may have impossibly high standards for yourself and others to live up to; but you find meaning where others cannot. Sometimes your nature is too selfish, and sometimes too sympathetic; in relationships it will be important to try to bring these extremes into balance and thus avoid the disappointments that come from misplaced or idealized affection.

You will often experience very clear flashes of understanding – like electrical impulses – which give you answers that have eluded you for weeks or months. Inspiration, too, comes in just such a way, and where some might be fearful of such sudden apprehensions, you will feel illuminated and enlightened. Your number is definitely one of courage and boldness – though take care not to over-stretch yourself, or place yourself under too much stress.

It will be important to find the right environment in which to learn about truth, and what is morally right for you. You will discard outworn ideas and find new paths to faithfulness, but you may also be forced to learn to be free from an overdependence on the material world. Through silence and serious thought, you will sift through the dross and understand what is valid. Your life is a call to be awakened, and you will broadcast your message to a wider audience through what you do.

Try not to worry when circumstances urge you to explore new territories. It is almost always your subconscious prompting you, goading you to new awareness and a deeper commitment to life. Whenever you feel thwarted or unsettled, contemplate your attitudes and ask what needs revising or reconsidering. You'll find yourself growing up and getting wiser and stronger to the end of your days.

You work hard to be fit and sensuous, but watch your health – you often push yourself without realizing! Stop when you are tired, to avoid making mistakes. You are a special soul with a marked awareness and a role to fulfil – one that will always be determined by your immense will.

6   5   4   3   2   1   9   8   7

Born on the 25th?

7 often retreats from others for the sake of stillness and 'apart-ness', but this number also gives you a stronger feeling for the needs and problems of others. You are especially prophetic and sensitive to what is unspoken – indeed a trait of number **7** generally, but expressed at its most vivid with your particular number. If other **7**s are more rational – or strive to be so – you have more pure clairvoyance and mysticism, but it doesn't make you flaky or unsound. You marry intellect with profound insight.

You must learn to trust your hunches and encourage your inner self to direct you. The understanding you have may have developed from your response to disappointment and the overcoming of unusual obstacles. Your family life may have been curtailed by outside dramas, or your chance to do what you wish tested by circumstance.

| 7 | 8 | 9 | 1 | 2 | 3 | 4 | 5 | 6 |

Often, though, this will simply mean you have to wait a little for the right opportunity to present itself, but as a result of feeling buffeted by fate in this way you may be highly charged emotionally, and moody without others understanding why. And yet, for all your emotional susceptibility, you tend to conceal your real feelings, and may be too reticent in expressing your needs. This frequently results in you being misunderstood, or feeling overlooked and unconsulted. You will need to find a way to say what you want or need without feeling guilty.

Seeing everything and saying nothing, you think long and hard before you speak. You are probably the closest observer at any event, and your insights are rarely founded on your own vision alone: you're able to put yourself in someone else's shoes and know how it feels to see the world their way, too. Excessive emotional response could affect your health and even blur your concentration, so work to relax and allow yourself to rest aloof from your sorrows at times. Try not to go over things again and again.

You are quite a perfectionist in whatever you spend your time and energies on, and perhaps the standards you set for yourself are too high – a little like those born on the 16th. This means you will be impossibly critical of yourself and those close to you. But unlike **7** or **16**, one of your faults is a lack of real faith in your ability. Do not underestimate yourself: you will constantly be surprised at your own achievements if you just make a start and dive in. Your talent is genuine.

You seem certain to be strongly inclined to music, with a natural gift for singing or playing an instrument. If you can learn to concentrate your efforts and believe in yourself you will prosper, but try not to sink into melancholy or moodiness, or even erratic behaviour, simply because you are so sensitive to the world around you. These are the negative trappings of your number if you do not lead a positive life, but if you focus on being positive you may be

7 8 9 1 2 3 4 5 6

the luckiest and best-achieving **7** of them all.

Your mind is alert and energetic, but you can nevertheless be truly happy leading a very simple life in an idyllic location, without needing luxury at all. Surrounded by books, a good record collection, and close to nature – '25's often prefer life in the country, or in a city space with a good-sized garden – you will find a redress to the stresses of overwork and perfect work standards, and you will succeed in any mentally demanding career where you can strive for excellence. Your skills and sense of space and light make you particularly drawn to the field of art, design and architecture; but you also have a facility for abstract thought, which makes you gifted working with computers, or teaching or painting. You may also enjoy – and excel at – woodwork or carving, writing and historical research. And, of course, true to your number, you too have that famous **7** nose which enjoys fine wine and food, perfume, and the cultivation of plants and flowers.

6   5   4   3   2   1   9   8   7

7 AT WORK

So, what kind of employee does your number make you? We've already seen that your birthday suggests you enjoy working with autonomy, or with just one or two close partners, but when you are in a large group, how do you fit in? If you're the boss, are you a good one? Which fields are likely to be the best for your talents? And which the worst? And what about the male/female divide? Is a 7 female boss more desirable than a 7 male colleague?

Here, we get to grips with your career potential, your needs and 'must-have's for job satisfaction, and your loves and loathes work-wise, hopefully highlighting some areas where there is room for you to adjust your manner around others, to help you achieve what it is you're aiming for.

In the marketplace

Your number might be deemed the 'I analyse' of numerology, rather like the astrological Earth sign Virgo, which is ruled by Mercury. This means that from the outset, in any field whatsoever, your mental focus and predisposition to apply yourself to the task in front of you should see you reach a level of distinction. It is that capacity to break down an awkward problem into manageable pieces, and to see what is beneath the surface, that gives you your edge.

You're definitely not a job-lot worker, or someone who takes the line of least resistance; you need good education and specialist training, so you can find a job you deeply care about. And if you feel you have lacked easy opportunities, you still have that determined streak that could make good use of libraries and the internet, or of mature-age degree courses, to fill in the gaps. We all benefit from a good education, but **7** only fulfils half of its potential without one.

6   5   4   3   2   1   9   8   7

INSIDE OUT

You will probably prefer to work in a smaller group, with people you can respect and trust, than in a large, faceless organization. Your natural abilities and willingness to learn about what is missing in your store of knowledge make you a reliable and invaluable colleague, but you will appreciate feeling valued by your team and, frankly, also wish to be left to get on with things under your own steam. **7**s never perform at their peak when they feel they're being watched, but free to find their own methods and make their own discoveries they will rarely disappoint. Your see beneath things, and to do this you must – as in life generally – have some quiet time. You must also feel you have an intelligent team who can discharge their brief ably, too.

The fields in which you can shine know no bounds. **7**'s talents make you an ideal researcher or writer, but equally that knack for analysis gives **7** the scientific mind to work in anything from medicine to engineering. Understanding the reason behind so many things, you have a kind of X-ray mind, and any work that involves the study or making of plans is perfect for you. Fields like chemistry and architecture, which both look at what happens below the surface, are as much in the talent sphere of a **7** as research, journalism, high-level teaching or stocks-and-shares dealing. The subjects seem disparate, but the common thread is the need to see how something is constructed *from the inside*, and to be able to break it down again to understand it.

WHERE DOES YOUR LIGHT REALLY SHINE?

Here are some of the qualities that **7**s bring to any job:

- Quick to see correlations, you are a gifted interpreter of information. This is true whether in relation to interpreting a coming fashion or business trend to analysing language and cultural meanings. The range of business opportunities that comes from this skill embraces everything from politics to marketing.

- Being artistic and a connoisseur of film and literature, **7**s can thrive in a vocation which puts such acute critical response to good use. It is this element of being the connoisseur, in fact, that also equips you for specialized knowledge of food and health, of wine and fine art.

- Always wanting to dig deeper, you are suited to being the specialist who can narrow down the exact information needed — or find the perfect bon mot for either teaching or analysing any creative project. **7**s also keep excellent notes and are able to predict just how much time or money will be involved in something creative: you look below the obvious, and are interested in what is hidden or neglected by other thinkers. More the PhD student than the broad educationalist, you must respect the minds of any members of your cohort; **7** is selective of company and obligations.

- The ability to fathom out what has not been articulated makes you interested in the law and all social policies.

Add to this **7**'s instinct for wanting to know the truth — and expecting be told it by others — and it is inevitable that your number often finds an excellent vocational stimulus in such an environment. Equally, the journalist digging for the truth behind a policy will be a **7**!

- Your natural refinement suits a career which provides beauty in the pared-down sense. Always eschewing garishness and ostentation, **7** as a host or a cook likes to prove the point that less is more. This manifests in any design or hospitality business as style leadership: **7** will go out on a limb to find the perfect balance between form and function, but always following taste that has nuance and is suggestive, rather than anything vulgar and too overt. Minimalism is usually **7**'s cup of tea.

- An ability to act as counsellor — but not as sycophant — makes you an invaluable aide where truth is needed for the sake of progress. If a flatterer is in demand, **7** is a poor choice, but if honest assessment and good advice is in order, no one could be better suited. Thus **7** may be a doctor, social worker or spiritual adviser in equal measure. **7** is a number that can offend many people in business, but when a **7** speaks it is usually worth hearing.

In any business or career, **7**'s wish is either to seek out the right person for a specific job or to be that person. Not comfortable with anyone who is a jack of all trades, **7** would make a world of properly trained individuals who are exactly tailored to do what they take on – making the possibility of perfection more a certainty than a matter of luck. Fields for which **7**s are especially suited include ...

Observation and analysis These aspects are at the root of much scientific and medical work, and the sciences are usually a strong point for you career-wise. The rule will be that – either in science or in medicine – you prefer to learn as much as possible in any one corner of the subject, making yours a number suited to being the surgeon or the diagnostician rather than the general practitioner. Any demanding branch of science will also suit the delving, focused mind of this intelligent number.

Music Music impregnates the air **7** breathes, and a career in the music industry would suit you well. Whereas a **6** or a **3** might suit a flexible niche in the market, **7** must be the soloist or the one-man/woman show. If you work in the business side of music, you will select and direct talent; in an orchestra, you will be the conductor of the first fiddle rather than of a session musician. If **7** is dedicated to a career in music, dedication is just what it will be.

Literature Although **7**s love the arts broadly, words are your strong point. Either in publishing – where you perfect the work of others and find its true marketplace – or in writing itself, **7** is truly at home. Work in journalism would be best for you if it were in specialized reporting or criticism; but you also have the instinct to write lengthy books. It is a loner's job to write for long hours, and research is invisible and vital behind every sentence. You have the exact character and focus to execute such work.

Law Truth-seeking **7** makes a superb lawyer. You can see exactly what's going on behind the apparent truth. Digging tirelessly until a clear picture emerges, a **7** makes a perfect specialist legal mind and may be drawn to criminal law, as it offers a platform for detective work, or to family law, where nobility of character and ability to communicate one-on-one with someone in need of counsel comes to the fore. Sometimes a conflation of law and writing, or law and medicine, might appeal to **7**'s wish to specialize.

Teaching **7**s are often found in the teaching profession, but prefer working with like-minded souls who are brighter than average. Thus, this makes you suited to the realms of university professors and higher specialists.

This list isn't exhaustive – 7s can shine in so many areas – but it does offer a taste of what kinds of field will most appeal to your number.

And for luck?

Whatever your work, you will achieve your maximum potential if you use a name to work with that includes the letters G, P or Y. Remember this when you are choosing a company name, if you go into business for yourself. It will help, too, for you to optimize your energy and positive attitude, if you decorate your work environment in the brick, russet and deep-red shades of early autumn. If you are going for an important interview, these colours would make a positive choice in your outfit, as they help you to project yourself in your most acute and intelligent light.

6   5   4   3   2   1   9   8   7

WORK PROFILE
The 7 female boss

Taking command of the situation when an unexpected visitor threatens chaos, the **7** woman in charge of her band keeps everyone **cool and confident**, and reminds them of what to focus on. No matter that no one was prepared for the international client's arrival, or that it was the day scheduled for rearranging the office, sorting through all the old files and having a general clear-out: the **7** female boss is **elegant** at all times, and primed in her deep sub-conscious for a possible emergency anyhow. Now, with well-groomed plain-coloured nails and an outfit that is so classical she could have worn it to the opera if required, she is quickly **up to speed** with all the details of the contract and ready to **dazzle** the impromptu guest with her sensible ideas that are so **stylishly presented**.

7   8   9   1   2   3   4   5   6

No one else will ever know how she knew just what questions would come up, or why the client had such unusual demands. Call it her **intuition**. And if all the males in the room were being subtly flirted with, they hardly noticed: she has them in a **vice-like grip**, because — with all of her tools of stylish personal presentation and **verbal charm** — it is her mind and her grasp of the details that has got her to the top, and it is very safe doing business with her.

Don't cross her, though! She has a **long memory** for hurts, and can't abide anyone challenging her view unless they are a **perfectionist** and specialist in their field to the same degree that she is. **Mildly arrogant**, and very prepared to go it alone when required, the 7 female boss is unafraid to say something unflattering to her peers, or to tell a partner they have lost the confidence or respect of the employees because they have been too preoccupied with their personal dramas. One thing's for sure: you'll never catch *her* making that mistake.

Of course, at home, her partner may be unsure how to **compete** with her work responsibilities – or, in fact, whether she'll even be home at any kind of sociable eating hour. When she is **focused**, she is indeed focused – and hard to deny anything to, as well!

WORK PROFILE
The 7 male boss

The tie is a little **distinctive**, the face intriguingly **sexy**. There might be a slight **boyish charm** – but his employees know better than to equate that to anything immature in the man himself. The **7** male boss has **substance** and – just like his female counterpart – **elegance**! Understated elegance is usually a feminine thing, but not with male **7**s, who have arrived at their harbour in command of the best ship in the navy. This man repudiates flashy behaviour from colleagues and underlings, but he has a wonderful sense of **humour** if you engage his brain in your witticisms. And, for everyone who wants to be in his good books – and who doesn't want that approbation? – the way to get there is to know your subject thoroughly and surprise him with your breadth of knowledge.

6   5   4   3   2   1   9   8   **7**

His desk is pared down to only what is required for a perfect day's work. Photos of his loved ones are unlikely to be anywhere on show, for he is too **private** for that. He may even be genuinely surprised at the effect he has on his female colleagues, because he's not really looking for it. But this man definitely **commands respect**, and he won't tolerate ignorance or ill-preparation from anyone – not even his peers right at the top of the game.

He has a reputation – justly deserved – for standing up for the **rights** of his junior team. He will never let anyone take the blame for an error unless they are actually responsible. If this means arguing with management, he is the lawyer to do it. He has an **impressive vocabulary**, an interesting way of researching private details about clients and co-workers, and is astonishingly fluent in his **knowledge** base. He has read so much, manages to be up-to-date about the world political picture, and cares about trying to make a product better and **fairer** – and healthier, if possible. 'Fair Trade' was probably his idea, but he won't boast about it. Mind you, he won't appreciate anyone else broadcasting his personal details, either.

It's not, perhaps, strictly accurate to say that his company adores him – for many are a little nervous of him, even though he is the most **approachable** person when there's a problem going on. He gives his admiration to others only where it is deserved, so fakes and lazy contributors won't last long in his domain. But he is **honest**, and his moderate praise means more than the generous effusions of his **3** or **6** co-bosses. And when you've won his attention and gained his admiration, his humour in the bar afterwards is a special reward. The **7** man in charge is **discerning** and **understated**, making him a person whose good opinion is **invaluable**. Just make sure his desk is organized and he can find exactly what he wants at a touch!

6   5   4   3   2   1   9   8   7

WORK PROFILE
The 7 female employee

Not the girl to chatter wildly in the ladies' room on her first day, the **7** female employee is **well-prepared** for what she might expect to have thrown at her. Just as she was impeccably prepared for her interview, having researched the taste and interests of her potential boss, so she could **impress**. Just as she was **smooth** at the interview for her college at university, when she moved seamlessly from her academic subject to the current political story to the exhibition that was just on at the oriental museum. She is always – *always* – **one step ahead**; and if she's not, she'll make you think she is.

When she starts out she will surprise everyone with her packed-lunch salad, or her handbag that contains a **treasure trove** of items that may (one day!) prove useful.

7   8   9   1   2   3   4   5   6

She won't trust the quality of the food on offer around the corner until she's done her **reconnoitre**, and she prefers real tea or coffee to anything instant or distilled in a fast machine. Her coffee mug has her own **marque** to distinguish it from anyone else's, and she'll wash it up properly before getting a refill.

Work is filed away in distinctive folders and box files that help her **organize** her space and her mind: this is one of her strong points. She can – and will – fit quite a lot into a day, but she prefers to be left to get one job **done properly** before she is asked to skip to another. Proper **concentration** is vital to her methods, and she will come up trumps every time – on the most obscure subjects – as long as she is allowed to find **her own way** of doing things. She will have her own **special contacts** and research places, and she knows where to go to find anything – from facsimile copies of Emily Dickinson's poetry to fleece-covered luggage to take to the Arctic Circle. She

6   5   4   3   2   1   9   8   7

is **resourceful**, **willing** and **good-humoured**.

And **impatient**! With any co-worker who wastes time chattering about what is unchanged from last week or last month, she has no tolerance. She wonders how some people even got their job – and she may have a point. Many other females will feel she is looking down her nose at them, but in truth she just prefers to make one or two really close friends and to be **cordial** and polite with the others. And, whoever her celebrity lovers were a few years ago, you are unlikely to find out about them – making her a **fascinating enigma**, or a **frustrating ally**. But it's worth being on her inner circle just for the privilege!

WORK PROFILE
The 7 male employee

Making a **significant impression** when he starts, with his better-than-average tailoring and his broad understanding of the company objective, the **7 male employee** is **never caught out**. He has a **personable** enough manner if he rates you as someone who is worth knowing, and his **intelligence** is clearly above the hoi polloi. He has taken trouble to know who is responsible for what, and, without being at all sycophantic, he is **astute** enough to make the right comment to the right person. All this, and his gun is barely smoking!

He may or may not be the one to go out for a game of squash with his co-workers before the day starts, but he is definitely a **good team-player** provided he has confidence in everyone's individual capacity. He doesn't waste

6   5   4   3   2   1   9   8   7

small talk on anybody, but he is **fair** and honest. He is slightly uncomfortable when he's on the rise through the ranks, because he is happiest when he is the specialized talent who knows the answers. **Whatever it takes** to get him to that phase, he'll do it.

He can be **relaxed**, sociable and **charming** when he likes you, but the work space is just as likely to be littered with **witty one-liners** at another's expense, if he thinks someone's not pulling their weight. And, without meaning to cause even the slightest offence, he'll give an **honest** answer when you ask whether the outfit you're wearing is suitable for that out-of-town client you have to entertain at the last minute – and it may not be what you want to hear! The risk with the **7** male employee is that, if you ask, you'll be told!

But isn't it lovely that he always smells so nice? And that his hair is properly cut? And that if he asks you to come around for a working dinner, he is not at all certain to have other things on his mind? With him, you get a little **class** and a lot of things to think about, and it's a bonus that he can really **cook** well, too. This is not the man to be caught with spinach in his teeth or dirty fingernails! Nor is he likely to ask anyone else to take the rap for him if he has missed something. He's in a hurry to get to the next level of **achievement** – not so much in an ambitious way as a 'let's all be adults in this world' kind of way.

If you need someone working next to you who pretends to love your taste in music, or not be hungry so you can eat the last piece of pizza, work with a **6** or a **9**. A **7** man is **modest yet arrogant**, shy yet outspoken on important issues, and definitely someone from whom everyone else can learn a lot about a **good work ethic**.

Ideal world or cruel world?
Best and worst jobs ...

IN AN IDEAL WORLD

Best job for a 7 female: Head of a fashion house specializing in couture (can hone exquisite taste and rise to the challenge of finding exactly the right look for demanding clientele, money no option)

Best job for a 7 male: Art dealer for international clients (pleasure of exploring and visiting works of art for a specialist market), or head of a surgical team in an elite hospital (for obvious reasons!)

IN A CRUEL WORLD

Worst job for a 7 female: Manager of a fast-food chain in an inner city (enjoys the responsibility but loathes the unhealthy food, lack of quiet and constant smell; the dishonesty of her position would hurt)

Worst job for a 7 male: Used card salesman (verbal skill wasted, and – unless it was a specialized dealership – no feeling of product integrity)

7'S CHILDHOOD

Seeing the way a number expresses itself in someone very young is fascinating, for the tendencies and responses are all in their infancy – and yet plain to see. Some facets of a number's power need to be grown into, and take time to reveal how they will be dealt with by the developing character. Sometimes the strength of a number can be a frustration when we're young.

If looking back on your own childhood through the lens of your number, you should discover – with considerable humour and irony – a renewed understanding of some of the difficulties or excitements you experienced. Or, if you have a child who is also a **7**, you may learn something more useful; it is an advantage to understand the qualities a number exudes over an awakening personality, especially in relation to talents and career strengths, as it might save a lot of frustrations. You'll be able to appreciate the positive traits, and handle negative ones more sympathetically.

Here, we take a detailed look at what it's like to be a child bearing your number. But what about the other numbers? Perhaps you have a child who is a **2**, and you'd like to know what that means? Or maybe you'd like to gain insight into friends' and siblings' childhoods, to see if it sheds any light on the people they have become today? A short profile is given for each number, along with advice for a **7** parent on dealing with other-number offspring.

Just as your own parents would have discovered when you were a child, the hardest thing with a **7** child is dealing with their intelligence and need for quiet space, and keeping them challenged. **7** children, as you know, need to be allowed to be a little bit adult, at all costs, and discounting their opinion or input frustrates them ...

The young 7

A child born on the 7th, 16th or 25th of any month must be nurtured as a future thinker! Even in primary school, this is a child with a focused mind and strongly developed critical sense. A **7** child is perceptive and, sometimes, disarmingly quiet. They will quite often prefer adult company, as their peers may seem too young and underdeveloped to them. Wise and difficult to know well, these are children with a serious cast to their intelligent mind, and they will appreciate others treating them with respect.

The fact that a **7** child can sit quietly and contemplate things deeply should not imply that they are introverted: quite the opposite. Though careful where to bestow their affections, **7**s are excellent friends when they choose someone they enjoy, and they can be dazzling company. A **7** will grow into a very good host, as long as the invited guests appeal, and they have a lovely sense of humour, which is apparent from their earliest years – even if it does sometimes find expression at others' expense. They will rarely be rude, but certainly have a good understanding of all that has been said – and what has not been. Listen to them capture those pithy expressions that characterize teachers, relatives and friends, with an unwavering ear and great humour; and take heed of their own impressions of the people they deal with! They will have a strong sense of who they can trust and who is only paying lip service to an opinion or belief. 7 children don't like such dishonesty.

All 7s as children have an inward reluctance to accept other people's ideas automatically – rather like 1; but there is a special propensity to independence in a child born on the 16th. This is the number of someone who finds it difficult asking for what they want, or even feeling that they have been consulted as to their own wishes. And all 7s have definite ideas about what to believe. They may not

7   8   9   1   2   3   4   5   6

7's toys

Encyclopedia • Scrabble • Chalk board • Chess • Solo musical instrument • Chemistry set • Ballet shoes • Tapestry kit • Microscope • Camera • Walking boots • Adult cookery book • Laptop computer • Computer games • Treehouse • Quality sound system • Oil paints

choose a conventional interest, but they will be spiritual and eclectic about what to give credence to.

7 children should be told the truth on virtually all matters. They will know if they are being deceived, and will respect being treated as an adult in any case – something that's especially easy for a 7 parent to do, as they have lived through such growing pains already. A 7 child's maturity can be unnerving, but you will respect their strength and drive to achieve expertise in what they enjoy. Take them to theatre productions when they are tiny and be prepared to be amazed at their devastating assessment of what was good and what was abysmal about the acting, staging or directing. A **7** cannot be duped into accepting the Emperor's New Clothes: if something is good they will say so, but they will never give way to popular or mass opinion if it is simply hyped. This is not unusual, perhaps, in a late teenager or someone in their early twenties discovering their powers; but with a **7**, these signs of independent critical assessment start much earlier. A **7** child gives any parent much to be proud of, both academically and in terms of humanitarian feelings.

School life has an importance for **7**s, and it is crucial to find the right environment in which a **7** can learn. A gifted teacher will lift this potentially high-IQ child out of a tendency towards irritation over subjects that may be perceived as a waste of time. A **7** needs to know why they are bothering to do something, and learning by rote, or simply because others do it, is never good enough. It is therefore essential – laying the foundations right from the start, for the whole direction of later life – that the right school and mentors be found, to excite a young **7** with their possibilities. Perhaps with this number more than any other, a lack of education will be detrimental. **7** has an enquiring mind, and must be shown how to channel it.

From early days, you will have a best friend in a **7** child. Discourage their bossiness – which comes from frustration with others – but allow them space and privacy. Here is a young soul who should never be bored with their own company.

The 1 child

This resourceful child has a different way of thinking, and will stand to one side and evaluate things without pressure. Repeat Grandma's sound advice on any subject to a **1** under the age of six, and they'll simply ask, 'Why?' Ignoring the social expectation to conform, **1** children often make us laugh with surprise.

A **1** child is tough and active – an inquisitive soul who wants to get on with things and not be held in check by others, however wise the parental eye might be. Stubborn and impatient, **1**s frequently suffer by questioning – though not from rudeness – the authority of a parent or teacher. **1**s break down tradition and find new ideas to form a fresh understanding of the world we're in. Your **1** child needs careful handling: a bright mind bursting with interest and disinclined to authority needs subtle direction. If **1** children dominate their friends and talk over their family it can make them socially inept and unable to co-operate in love relationships later in life, leading to loneliness rather than just self-reliance.

A **1**'s greatest challenge is to learn to live in a social world and understand that they are not inevitably right. To foster a **1**'s unique personality and avoid insensitivity to others, let them behave like an adult. This confidence a **1** child will ably repay. **1** children suffer from being misunderstood, as they're often so happy in their private hours and so demanding of having their own time that they may not learn to express their need for others. The seeds are sown early as to how to approach another person for signs of affection, and an equally self-reliant **7** parent may not be able to show them; however, it is certain that the two of you will share very close one-on-one time, and this will help. You will definitely never cosset your **1** too much – but do give them a cuddle sometimes!

The 2 child

All children born on the 2nd or 20th need affection and a peaceful environment to grow up in. Those born on the 11th or 29th are a little different, being master number **11**s with **2** as the denominator, and they have an old head on young shoulders from the start. But even they – for all their drive toward excitement and adventure – will be happiest if their home life is mostly secure and tranquil.

These highly sensitive and intuitive children know what you will say before you say it. They are also dreamy and process ideas in their sleep, waking to instinctive and wise solutions to their problems. But they are vulnerable, and need reassuring more than most numbers. They are acutely sensitive to criticism, feeling that all comments are proof that they're not quite good enough, so you need to deliver your words with tact and an awareness of their needs.

| 7 | 8 | 9 | 1 | 2 | 3 | 4 | 5 | 6 |

2 children are talented artists, actors, dancers and/or musicians: they know how others *feel*. A **2** child prefers to support friends and family as often as possible, and this can make them a doormat ready to be walked on unless those they live with are alert to their inclinations. If the **2** is an **11**, the wish to help out will be very strong indeed, but these children also have a finely tuned moral sense and will be offended by injustice – especially against them! Don't dish out judgement until you have all the facts.

2s are good healers and can make others feel better – even from their earliest years. Knowing when to cuddle or touch and when to be quiet, they often have a stillness that works miracles around the sick, the sad and the elderly. A **7** parent will reciprocate and respect this ability to heal and see below the surface, although a **2** child needs some demonstrativeness, which may be forgotten by someone so self-reliant. You will come to enjoy the affection and quiet support you receive from your gentle, intelligent **2**.

6   5   4   3   2   1   9   8   7

The 3 child

From the cradle, **3**s hold parties and like to mix with other children. They have a capacity to laugh and precipitate laughter, even when things go a little wrong. **3** children are like the reappearing sun after rain, and their energies can be restorative for everyone. Creative and playful, nothing keeps them low for long.

Like a juggler keeping plates and balls in the air, **3**s have several activities and talents on the go from the start. This can be a problem, however: making decisions is hard for them, and they need a wise older counsellor who can talk out the options and give them room to think. Even then, a decision once reached can always be changed – and a **3** child will find a way to run in several directions at one time.

Keep your **3** busy with lots of artistic activities, using

7   8   9   1   2   3   4   5   6

colours and textures — right from babyhood — to open their eyes to what they can do. Even before the age of ten a strong personal taste will begin to develop — and it may not be the same as their parents'. Using up their flow of energy on a multitude of tasks will be demanding on both parents, but the **3** child does give a great deal back in return.

3s are talkers and have a witty repartee, even when tiny: you'll be surprised at what you hear from them sometimes, and will wonder where it came from. Naturally gifted at PR, they will talk you around when you are set against one of their wishes, but you will need to direct them now and again or nothing will ever be finished! A **7** parent with a **3** child may feel a headache coming on at times, but must give the **3** freedom to experiment, and try not be upset when they are messy, or chatter too much. Give them time to grow, and accept that they may not have your stillness or focus. They have a way of coming back smiling.

The 4 child

Surprisingly insecure and in need of praise, these children are reliable and hard-working and want to do well. They are their own worst critics at times, second only to number **7** children, and they glow when appreciated. They are happiest with family around them – even extended members – and often prefer holidays in familiar places. That said, they can be very quiet and self-sufficient when required, for they concentrate well.

These are organized children who won't cope well if their parents aren't as organized as they are! Never lose a school form or an item from their games kit on a crucial day, as this will cause them serious panic. They like to have material possessions around them because this bolsters their feeling of security, and will manage their pocket money well, content to do odd jobs and chores to gain this reward.

| 7 | 8 | 9 | 1 | 2 | 3 | 4 | 5 | 6 |

4s love the earth and buildings. They will treasure a patch of garden given them to tend, or a garden house they can extend or build outright. If they are born on the 22nd, rather than the 4th, 13th or 31st, they will truly have architectural talents, and may follow design as a career later. All **4** children, though, are handy at craft work and excellent at projects which require intelligence combined with method to get something done. They hate being late and don't admire tardiness in others, either.

As children, **4**s are loyal and dependable to family and friends, and are more patient than many numbers. They will make light of complex tasks, but they need to be allowed to do things in their own way. A **7** parent will be both frustrated by their **4** child's more plodding way of doing things but also thrilled by their ability to concentrate for hours and see a task to the end. **7**'s good teaching skills and **4**'s focus blend well, and you admire their tenacity. The relationship will grow stronger with time.

The 5 child

Unable to be confined or sit still, a **5** child is bursting with curiosity. Very sociable and happy to be on the move, these adventurous youngsters have much in common with **1**s, but are more willing to work in a team, and good at picking up on other people's ideas, only to improve them.

From their first few words, **5** children have good memories and a facility for speech – they speak and learn quickly, and can pick up more than one language. Even more physical than **1**s (although the two numbers are alike in this), they are excellent at sport or physical co-ordination. They chatter, are full of energy, and like to play to an audience. But most importantly, **5** children love to be free – to explore, laze, hunt, create, discover and travel. Take your **5** child away on holiday and they quickly make friends with others, and acquire a taste for foreign places. They will

7   8   9   1   2   3   4   5   6

even experiment with different food, if you're lucky.

5s find a reason to slip away if they're bored with adult company — so don't be offended. Their minds can pursue several streams of active interest, so they need a great deal of amusement to stretch them. This adventurous spirit can be a worry to their family sometimes and, indeed, 5s need to understand house rules about asking first, or telling someone where they're off to. The difficulty is that 5 children usually don't want to explain themselves to anyone.

The test for a 5's parent is to set their child constructive challenges that will vent their curiosity in good ways. 5s will pick up technology and music (other forms of language, in a sense) quickly, but they don't like dull routine work — which will irritate a 4 sibling if they have one. A 7 parent of a 5 will need to let them do their own thing, but will hate their restlessness and noise, and how they dip into many interests. But you will recognize their talents and creativity, so be patient while they grow up a little.

The 6 child

Here's a young soul in need of a peaceful haven, just like a **2**, but a **6** will literally feel ill if there is dissension around them. Always wanting to beautify their surroundings and make pretty presents for Mum, these talented, sensitive children have many gifts for creative expression. They will also nurse the sick cat or anyone who needs gentle kindness, but are not always robust themselves, and should be sheltered from bad weather or aggressive viruses.

As children, **6**'s musical talents should emerge – and they often have beautiful speaking or singing voices. They are also the peacemakers of the family – natural creators of balance and harmony. Give them a free hand with their bedroom and their flower garden, and be ready to learn from them. Both boys and girls usually make good cooks when they are older, too, so time spent in the kitchen won't be wasted. Birthday presents that foster their good eye — a camera or set of art tools — will usually fit them well.

Despite being sensitive to others and quite intuitive, **6** as a child is a little shy and needs drawing out — especially if there has been much change in their young life, because **6** children need stability and like to remain a tiny bit traditional. They become very attached to their home. But if their family life is unconventional they will ultimately adjust, because they offer their family a lot of love, and like to be shown love in return. Even the boys have a feminine side which in no way calls their gender into question.

Good at school and almost as well-organized as **4**s, this is a number which needs time to grow into itself: **6**s are enormously talented. A **7** parent will be gentle and fairly patient with a **6**, who is artistic and intuitive in many similar ways. **6** is more sociable and people-needy, but a **7** should be flexible enough to allow a stream of friends through the door, in the interests of their pretty, gentle **6**.

6   5   4   3   2   1   9   8   7

The 8 child

Here we have a young executive in the making. Even when they are still at school these children have a canny nose for what will make good business – and yet they are generous, hard-working and prepared to learn everything it will take to succeed in this life. Children born on the 8th, 17th and 26th like to have charge of their own finances, and to be given scope to do 'grown-up' activities – organizing their own parties and making arrangements for outings with their friends.

These children have strength and energy, but mentally are reflective and wise, too. They always see both sides to an argument – so parents who ask them to choose sides, beware! An **8** makes good judgements, and even before the age of ten they have a sense of what is fair and what is morally right.

| 7 | 8 | 9 | 1 | 2 | 3 | 4 | 5 | 6 |

As this number rules the octave, many **8** children are extremely musical and have a wonderful sense of rhythm. This last even assures they can be good at sport, as it takes innate timing to perfect many physical skills. **8**s also like philosophical ideas and relish being given 'big concepts' to chew over, especially concerning politics or religious ideas. **8**s are proud, and like to research things carefully – so as long as they are not bored, you will find an **8** child with their head in a book or on the internet, or watching programmes that educate and broaden their vistas.

An **8** child is always striving for enlightenment and a challenge, like you, though you must be pragmatic when they inevitably pull in the opposite direction. Though independent, they are loyal to those they love, and a delicate sensibility makes them look at the other side of a story, or fight for an underdog. You understand this humanism very well, and mostly you will respect the exceptional qualities, spirituality and mind of your philosophical, driven **8**.

The 9 child

Here is a person born for the theatre, or to travel the world and befriend everyone. **9**s have an expansive view, and don't like to be restricted. With a good head for science and the arts, there are many career directions a **9** may take, so parents will have their work cut out trying to help them choose. However, because the number **9** is like a mirror, with every number added to it reducing again to that same number (for example: 5+9 = 14, and 1+4 = 5), **9** children are able to take on the feelings of just about anyone, which is why they are so artistic and good at drama and writing.

From their first years in school it will be clear a **9** child has a wonderful dry sense of humour and a taste for the unusual. **9** children are not often prejudiced and seem to be easy-going – though they are sensitive to the atmosphere around them, picking up vibes like a sponge. If you

7 8 9 1 2 3 4 5 6

speak to them harshly they will take it seriously, and are protective of others who seem to be hurt in this way too.

9s have a delicate relationship with their parents, but particularly with the father figure. A **9** girl will want to idolize her dad, and will feel desperately disappointed if circumstances are against this, while a **9** boy may wish to emulate his father – and yet they often grow up without enough input from this important person, who is busy or away. A **9** child must be wise ahead of their time, and so this lesson is thrown at them in one guise or another.

The **7** parent of a **9** child needs to be more broadly hospitable, allowing a stream of **9**'s friends and interests through the door. Your **9** appreciates your intelligence and work ethic, as well as your humanitarian side, and recognizes your pride in them and concern for their brilliant future, rewarding you with affection and kindness. Grown-ups from the start (like you), their philosophical mind and willingness to keep the peace fills you with admiration.

6   5   4   3   2   1   9   8   7

7 AT PLAY

We have discovered how your number expresses itself through your character in relation to your family and your general personality, what instinctive reactions go with your number in everyday situations, and how it might shape your career path and colour your childhood. But every day our DAY number also influences the way we respond to the social world around us. So, what can it say about our leisure hours? Is yours a number that even allows itself to relax? (Well, you probably already have some answers to this one!) What can your number reveal about the way you like to spend your time, or how you achieve pleasure outside of duty?

Over the next few pages we take a look at what makes you tick, as a **7**, when you are unwinding – and how **7**s prefer to fill their time, if given a choice. Let's see whether you're typical in this respect ... And who knows – if you haven't already tried all the activities and pastimes mentioned, maybe you'll get a few ideas about what to put on your list for next time!

The 7 woman at play

Through myriad interests and an energy graph that peaks at times of pressure and troughs only when permitted to, it should be clear by now that a **7** taking leisure is a precarious thing. Sometimes, a **7** woman's ideal pleasure is just to take one human being with her to a spa to say … nothing to! This is a special kind of being – someone with whom you can totally relax without the need for words. But at other times, your leisure time is fed by fast and furious exchanges that demonstrate a rapid-fire wit and cynicism. A special companion is required for that one, too!

7 girls, in truth, have a rainbow-coloured spectrum of turn-ons in their leisure time. Reading a newspaper can be bliss if it represents a catch-up with the world, for recharging a **7**'s mental battery is as important for a woman as a man. In some respects, there is little gender divide for this number – the men being just as fussy about details, and the women just as 'masculine' in their enquiring intellect. So, you'll spend your chill-out time replenishing your mental stores as diligently as your male counterpart. This means books, documentaries, new cinema releases and current exhibitions all represent that hybrid of leisure and business for a **7** woman. Relaxation is – usually – also a challenge. Oh, except on those spa days!

An ideal weekend for you might well be heading into the countryside to ransack antique shops, browse book markets or sample local wineries. You'll know all about the area long before you get there, and what you don't know already you will pick up through attentive listening to locals and close attention to public notices. Gently astute, you're always looking for what will appeal to your gathering mind. You'll know the best place to get a quiet slice of hedgerow cake, or the bistro where the live jazz is good. Any and all of these passions pepper the female **7**'s free time, and those who love you will indulge your need for solitude — and even that intrigue for such specialized interests that almost borders on obsessive/compulsive behaviour! You must have your cheese from the right place, your berries from the organic farm, and your fish from the man whose story you hear as he unloads it from the trawler in the quaint fishing village. **7** ladies listen well, and they get others to talk when they aren't in a hurry.

Like a **6**, you may choose to spend several hours at an easel or with sketching materials, for art could be a very serious passion for you. Unlike **6**, though, if you take up painting or quilt-making you will become *really* good at it, because while **6** is relaxed about what they like, happy to be a dilettante, **7** has a different view, and wants to get better and better at something over time. If your children are along for the ride, you'll teach them carefully and give them your full attention until your passion for perfection is theirs too. I am not sure if it is possible to inherit a number, as it were, but if it is so, then a **7** is the one who will pass on their habits almost unnoticeably. The **7** mum on vacation may use a large part of it to read to, and with, her family: shared joys with just a very select group are her pleasure.

When the luggage is taken down from the attic for a trip, chances are a **7** woman will revisit a place where she has been happy before. This is not because you are lacking curiosity about new vistas, but because of the genuine pleasure you take from a deeper acquaintance with the places you know. Where a **5** or a **3** may not buy a holiday cottage because of the implication of being tied down, a **7** can discover endless new lights in which to view a familiar place. So there you may be, independently putting in a bid for that cottage on the river, decorating it with light colours, mesmerized by the tranquil view at the end of the long day. Work and rest are intrinsic to a **7**'s life, as well as their leisure.

The 7 man at play

If he is more than fifty years old, he is situated in his study or living space with his favourite books and a glass of fine red wine, with a good fire blazing if the weather permits. If he is younger than this, he still masters an unhurried look – a convincing portrait of someone oozing leisure hours, while his mind is intractably combing a document or a newspaper for more information.

A **7** man always manages to look cool and controlled – even when busy absorbing facts at a rate of knots. You do this in company, too, and your companions have no idea they are being so successfully scrutinized, for you look so relaxed! And you know how to relax well. Movies are a passion, as are books: but, unlike a **6**, who loves the visual treat, or a **5**, who is fascinated by the action, or a **3**, who loves drama for the chance to copy or outdo the best lines, a **7** man with a book or cinema habit is enjoying the *intellectual* ideas presented.

You may therefore be inclined to look down a little on what you might call 'generic fluff' – the more popular reading lists and bestsellers, or the box office winners. You're more likely to while away an evening at an art-house cinema or in the biography section of the bookshop. You will almost certainly prefer non-fiction to fiction eight times out of ten, but will simply read what you consider to be good literature. You are decidedly unaffected by popular taste, and unconcerned with anyone else's opinion – except as a spur to a lively debate (which you will probably win hands down). Such a gifted critic – with an eye for the flaws – you are difficult to debate with.

Quiet trips away are a staple diet for the **7** man at rest – just as they are for a **7** woman. You will enjoy spa days, as well – as long as they're not accompanied by too many New Age-y dolphin noises or too much chit-chat from the therapist. **7** men are surprisingly 'female' without being in the least feminized, with a liking for very clean skin and nails, and for fine shoes and sensuous fabrics. Weekends in health resorts will definitely appeal, especially if there is a chance to escape to a historic city or a deserted beach at break times.

When a **7** man has free time – similarly to a **7** woman – it is likely he will make some use of it to improve a talent or an interest. If you are into cooking (which is almost certain to be true), you will contemplate a week in a Tuscan kitchen on a cookery course, or a day at a fish restaurant under the tutelage of a master. If you know your wines, you may decide to pedal off to France so that you can know them better; or, if you have a good command of writing, you may wish to hone your literary skills on a weekend retreat. And if you're excited by herbs and landscape gardening (also very likely), you will do a crash course to learn how to make more use of them, or grow a wider range or fruiting plants, or learn to propagate.

Leisure for a **7** – man or woman, in truth – is actually a mental approach to life: to enjoy what you do every day, and do it as often as possible.

7 IN LOVE

Love: it's what we all want to know about.
What's your style as a lover? And your taste —
where does that run? Do you want a partner who
is, ideally, as discriminating and as private as you?
Or would you rather have a love in your life who
is more outgoing, adding balance to your quiet
intensity? Everything about you says 'taste' and
'discernment', but is this also the case when
it comes to your love life?

Our first task is to consider how you see others as potential partners, and what you are likely to need from them. Why are you attracted to someone in the first place? This is where we begin ... But then you might like to pass the book across to your other half (if you have one), for the second subject of discussion is: why are *they* attracted to *you*? What does it mean to have a **7** lover?

Telltale traits of the 7 lover

- Aristocratic and, therefore, enigmatic
- Full of alluring secrecy
- Intelligent, and always one step ahead of their partner
- Can be very bossy in a relationship
- Expects perfection
- Sometimes hard to know what they want or need or feel
- Must have space

How do you do?
A 7 IN ATTRACTION

At any gathering, **7** shines. This is not through overt charisma, or noise, or a bubbly personality, as with the **3**s and
the **5**s, or through sensual beauty, like the **6**s. **7** has a way,
at the point of introduction, of making others feel their
power quietly. Instead of broadcasting their witticisms
across the dance floor or during the theatre intermission,
they speak with quiet authority to a select gathering,
which makes interested newcomers want to get up closer
and listen. **7**s charm their quarry with understatement
that seems to say, 'If you want to know me, you'll have
to come to me on my terms.' It is this amazing mix of
alertness and apparent indifference that is so compelling.
Whether they are male or female, standing or regally
seated, the **7** exudes a message that they are keenly atten-

tive and yet hyper-relaxed. And what are you looking so intently at, in other people?

7s are very choosy in relationships. You want the best on the market – in whichever way you judge that 'best'. Usually it is someone who also emits an aura of independence and confidence. **7** is drawn to its antithesis in relationships, more than to someone who is cut from the same cloth. You will definitely admire somebody with wit and intelligence – that much is essential; but you may find that the loner/independent type who excites you is also someone who makes you feel that you will never completely discover their whole, secret self. You will have work to get to know them over many years. A part of their hurt, pain, sorrow, joy, disappointment may be withheld, and you will find that fascinating. You will also admire someone who is a little flamboyant, being the opposite of your own style: but you will never countenance anyone who is giddy or shallow.

6   5   4   3   2   1   9   8   7

Mind over matter

In a physical relationship, a **7** will be turned on by their lover's mind and physical grace as much as anything to do with their body. Of course, a **7** man is as attracted to a beautiful woman as any other number would be, but there is a difference. **7** will look deeper, and see what is beautiful to the mind; it may be that a **7** man is excited by a woman whose beauty is more surreal, or intelligent, or striking. He will fall for her dignity far more than her dazzle. And a **7** woman will find a man sexy if he has conversation and learning, and a different take on the world. **7**s of both sexes are snobs – intellectual or otherwise – and anyone who seems cheap or flashy will have to find a different lover to snare!

As a **7**, you need a partner who is also good company, for you will choose again and again to spend your own time with just the closest circle. Only if there is not enough

7   8   9   1   2   3   4   5   6

intellectual overlap will you find it necessary to fill your time with many others socially – and this is a sign that things probably won't last. A **7** needs a lot of independent time away from their love, and, when together, they need someone who can be quiet and content without pestering them for reassurances of their feelings. A **7** is looking for that person who'd be comfortable on a desert island with them. Only self-reliant and interesting people need apply.

Setting the standard

The date that convinces a **7** things might go further is the date who can be equally poised. Anyone who needs to strut their stuff and show off will be dropped home without a coffee. The lover whose eyes say more than their voice box has an excellent chance of creating that allure **7**s hunger for. So many people are attracted to a **7**'s stillness and intelligence because they need to rely on it; a **7** falls for the person who doesn't quite need them.

And that love who will steal your heart is the one who may not be a permanent gallery visitor but who will look at all new things with enthusiasm. It will be someone who can leave you to Mozart or Monteverdi when your 'Do Not Disturb' sign is hung out. And it will be someone who is equally clever – albeit in a totally different area or direction. After the first passion, **7** needs a partner who is very much a friend and a spiritual soul, not too hung up on material goods, always ready to learn something more. **7** must, in short, find a partner capable of living up to their standards – which are discerning. And if this means having an off-campus lover who is only there on weekends, fine. Why not?

But now, what does a lover see in you? That's easy: a challenge!

To have and to hold?

LOVING A NUMBER 7

Who can help loving this extraordinary person – this closed book with an intelligent mind and seeming unconnectedness with much of the world's concerns, their head in a book or a cloud?

A man is drawn to a **7** woman for such an array of things. After just a short time with her, you will have realized how much like those proverbially deep 'still waters' she is. Her elegance and social confidence (while giving the impression that she is just a little bit 'above' everyone around her) were apparent from the start. If you met her in the office, she'll have impressed you by being willing to take on anybody – at any level – and put them right when they are wrong. If you met socially, she quite simply stood out from other people, with a distinctive voice, and

6   5   4   3   2   1   9   8   7

clothes that looked spectacular in a quiet and not necessarily 'à la mode' way. Her crisp and classic scent spelled 'class' from the first.

And after a year, do you know her much better? To surprise her on her birthday, you may have learned that anything from tickets to Paris to a good pair of hiking boots would be almost guaranteed to bring a dry-humoured smile. In her romantic spirit, a **7** lover is an aficionado of anything from poetry and painting to a nature trail, from a city break in a metropolis of first-rate galleries to a weekend in a tiny fishing village on the coast. And in any of these places, walking is heaven. If the **7**'s would-be lover has done the right research, they will know that anyone who loves a **7** must have good feet and leg muscles: walking is vital head-clearing, thinking time for a **7**, and a romantic weekend arranged around this need should score well on brownie points. (Incidentally, both the poet William Wordsworth and his sister Dorothy, a writer, were **7**s.)

And if the **7** girl with the inventive, attentive lover is fortunate enough to be near the sea, this might take precedence over a walk. She will light up for the potential partner who can sail, surf or swim with her. This means, of course, that when wooing a **7** woman, the successful admirer will do better to offer her some watery space to be near, or perhaps some country lanes to stroll down, as a backdrop to growing intimacy. Not that walking the length of the Champs Elysées on a luxury shopping trip is heinous for a **7** girl – who will be delighted to be spoiled by a lover with Parisian tokens of his rising affection; but this alone is not enough, as it doesn't have quite the same fascination for her as it would for a **3** or **2**, or an **8**. **7** would rather be lost in thought – literally – with a lover whose mind she likes, someone who intrigues her with unexpected turns in his character. In any relationship, a **7** can never be bought and paid for.

6   5   4   3   2   1   9   8   7

Less is more

And this is equally true for the woman who falls for a **7** man. If you have started to surrender your heart to a man who is a **7**, you must be prepared for a sometimes lonely road. Turn back now, if you're that person who needs to be told constantly how much you are beloved. The **7** man feels that less is more in all things, and this is true with a lover, too. He may admire your handling of clients or family members who don't eat dairy, or don't like to sit near a door: but, however smoothly you deal with these hiccups, you will need to infer all compliments from the merest gestures.

He is only with you at all because you are *exceptional* in his mind, and this must be enough. To be near him you have proven that you have grace and humour, that you are clever and self-contained, that you are a good listener and that you are able to give him essential privacy without being too clingy. Large gestures or romantic outpourings won't come from this man.

But male or female, a **7** is quite vulnerable underneath, and patience may repay their lover over time. As for the sex: that quiet physicality that is sexy because it is governed by that fascinating mind is truly an aphrodisiac in both **7** men and women. He, or she, is very aware of what is special about them, and – as far as they're concerned – you can take them or leave them. Somehow a **7** lover can bring out all of the best or all of the worst in their partner, and anyone lacking self-worth will struggle. But there is no one as discerning on the planet, and it will be a test of character for anyone to really awaken their love. **7** is reticent in relationships: if you love one, be prepared to learn everything from scratch, and apply no other 'rules' to this love affair.

6   5   4   3   2   1   9   8   7

7 in love

Turn-ons:

- ♥ ✔ A partner who is emotionally self-sufficient, with good self-discipline
- ♥ ✔ Someone who is well-read with an independent cast of mind
- ♥ ✔ A lover who can leave some things unsaid
- ♥ ✔ A partner in exploration and philosophical thought

Turn-offs:

- ♥ ✘ A needy soul who must have constant reassurance
- ♥ ✘ Someone who is jealous of the vital time spent apart
- ♥ ✘ A person who is insecure, or who carries the expectation that love must go according to certain recognized moves and rules
- ♥ ✘ Anyone brash or uninformed

7'S COMPATIBILITY

In this weighty section you have the tools to find out how well you click with all the other numbers in matters of the heart, but also when you have to work or play together too. Each category opens with a star-ratings chart, showing you – at a glance – whether you're going to encounter plain sailing or stormy waters in any given relationship. First up is love: if your number matches up especially well with the person you're with, you will appreciate why certain facets of your bond just seem to slot together easily.

But, of course, we're not always attracted to the people who make the easiest relationships for us, and if you find that the one you love rates only one or two stars, don't

6   5   4   3   2   1   9   8   7

give in! Challenges are often the 'meat' of a love affair — and all difficulties are somewhat soothed if you both share a birthday number in common, even if that number is derived from the *total* of the birth date rather than the actual DAY number. In other words, if your partner's LIFE number is the same as your DAY number, you will feel a pull towards each other which is very strong, even if the DAY numbers taken together have some wrinkles in their match-up. You will read more about this in the pages that follow the star chart.

The charts also include the master numbers **11** and **22**: these bring an extra dimension to relationships for those whose birth-number calculations feature either of these numbers at any stage. (For example, someone with a DAY number of **2** may be born on the 29th: 2+9 = **11**, and 1+1 = **2**. This means you should read the compatibility pairings for your number with both a **2** and an **11**.)

Sometimes the tensions that come to the surface in

7   8   9   1   2   3   4   5   6

love relationships are excellent for business relationships instead: the competitiveness that can undermine personal ties can accelerate effectiveness in working situations. We'll take a look at how other numbers match up with yours in vocational situations. And, when it comes to friends, you'll see why not all of your friendships are necessarily a smooth ride ...

In all matters – whether love, work or friendship – you will probably discover that the best partnerships you make involve an overlap of at least one number that you share in common. A number **7** attracts other number **7**s in various close ties throughout life.

NOTE: To satisfy your curiosity, ALL numbers are included in the star charts, so that you can check the compatibility ratings between your friends, co-workers and loved ones – and see why some relationships may be more turbulent than others!

| 6 | 5 | 4 | 3 | 2 | 1 | 9 | 8 | 7 |

Love

YOUR **LOVE** COMPATIBILITY CHART

	1	2	3	4	5
With a 1	★★★★	★★★★★	★★	★★★	★★★★★
With a 2	★★★★★	★★★★	★★★	★★★★★	★
With a 3	★★	★★★	★★★★★	★★	★★★★
With a 4	★★★	★★★★★	★★	★★★★	★★
With a 5	★★★★★	★	★★★★	★★	★★★
With a 6	★★★	★★★★	★★★★	★★★	★★
With a 7	★★★★★	★★	★★★	★★★★★	★★★
With an 8	★★★★	★★★★	★★★★★	★★★	★★★
With a 9	★★★	★★★	★★★★★	★★	★★★
With an 11	★★★★	★★★★	★★	★★★★★	★★
With a 22	★★★★	★★★★★	★★★	★★★★	★★★★

7   8   9   1   2   3   4   5   6

6	7	8	9	11	22
★★★	★★★★★	★★★★	★★★	★★★★	★★★★
★★★★	★★	★★★★	★★★	★★★★	★★★★★
★★★★	★★★	★★★★★	★★★★★	★★	★★★
★★★	★★★★★	★★★	★★	★★★★★	★★★★
★★	★★★	★★★	★★★	★★	★★★★
★★★★★	★	★★★	★★★★★	★★★★	★★★★
★	★★★	★★★★	★★★	★★★★	★★★★★
★★★	★★★★	★★★	★★	★★★★★	★★★★
★★★★★	★★★	★★	★★★	★★★★	★★★
★★★★	★★★★	★★★★★	★★★★	★★	★★★★★
★★★★	★★★★★	★★★★	★★★	★★★★★	★★

6	5	4	3	2	1	9	8	7

7 in love with a 1   ★★★★★

This is a marriage of true minds, in a way. You have so many character traits in common that it seems inevitable you will attract each other. Better yet, you attract each other's good qualities! Your enigmatic reserve and intelligence are a magnet for **1**, who seems to reach into their most spiritual inclinations when you come together.

The **1** will need to curb their propensity to say exactly what they think without pausing for thought, because **7**s think very deeply and analytically, and will question **1**'s more impulsive reactions. They risk your wrath if they appear to be brash or crude. Also, if they are too demanding, they will lose you: as loners too, they should recognize your need for keeping some corners of your personality from everybody – even from the love of your life. **1** is private, too, but may feel that there is a well of pain, experience or loneliness which lies behind your complex nature, and your **1** may never be allowed to go there. They must be patient about this, for it isn't personal. Yet, if they can wait, they may be ultimately rewarded with your greater confidence. **7**s speak in their own time!

1 is a born extrovert, but you are a little bit introverted – in some departments, at least. Even if you have another more outgoing number as your LIFE number (*see page 214*), you still build a wall of silence around you in relationships. Family memories and early shaping experiences cast a long shadow. You need your **1** lover to be aware of your depth, your need for truth and honesty, but also your desire for independence. Some of these ideas seem contradictory – yet they are all true. If a relationship between you is to work, your **1** will have to cultivate more patience than they usually show, and be a tasteful and generous lover.

One of the qualities your **1** most admires is your shrewd brain and inner poise and dignity: the poise comes, in fact, from a capacity to see into people and into things so profoundly, and with such serenity. You, in turn, will admire your **1**'s sharp mind and originality, for **7**s are in many ways intellectual snobs who can't be bothered with uneducated minds, and this will suit a **1**, more often than not. As a pair, you will have a house of books and music, wine and – possibly – antiques. Although your **1** likes many modern things, you shares their taste for one-offs. This can lead to some very interesting journeys together – both metaphysical and actual.

Your physical relationship may be excellent. A **7** lover will have more composure than a **1**, whose energy may at times seem exhausting, but this is potentially a very powerful and empathetic relationship. Both of you focus well, and know what you want. Each of you has an attractive amount of self-reliance and individuality which excites the other one. You are both clever loners, and you will find enough to occupy you in one another if you can just give each other an inch here or there.

The **1** must try to meet you halfway on your standards of health and neatness: **7** can never be happy living in a messy apartment, and functions best in an environment that is elegant and precise. In fact, probably the worst problem for the **1** to negotiate is that you can be so critical of everything and everyone – especially of yourself – and **1** is sensitive to criticism. Don't let the organization of the space you share together become a matter of contention.

Key themes

Both have very original taste – you generate a stunning home atmosphere • Spur each other's creative concepts • **1** strains against **7**'s perfectionism • Intelligent conversations • Private time shared between you well

6   5   4   3   2   1   9   8   7

7 in love with a 2   ★★

This relationship has a little more potential than the star rating might suggest – but is not an obvious success. What is good between you is that there is a chance of arriving at a harmonious day-to-day existence without much friction, but this can be a problem too. **2** and **7** may not make much progress in life together, and **7** is never an easy prospect for gentle **2**, who is unlikely to push hard enough for what they want. Thus, as the partnership-minded member of the love affair, **2** has to think that what may work best for tranquillity, at times, is solitude: **7** requires a great deal of time alone. If not given this physically, you will demand it by withdrawing from your **2**, even when sharing the same room – which can be very frustrating for them.

And you, enigmatic **7**, will almost never tell **2** what's on your mind. **7**s keep secrets out of habit, and your **2** may not like that at all. Their famous intuition will need to work overtime. But what they will do is respect your excellent mind and your exquisite but rather unusual taste, and find a kind of compulsion in believing they have a duty to drag you out of being unhappy or on your own – when there are times they should just leave you well alone. Sometimes they make the mistake of feeling that silence between you is serenity, because they want it so much; often, this quiet is a disguise for things that you feel are wrong, and won't express. Read: danger zone.

The **2** is likely to be more of an extrovert around you than with many other numbers, for **7**'s moody nature forces **2** forwards, and you appreciate **2**'s charm and gentleness – even seek their seemingly calm manner with people – because it is not your own way. You are so witty, perhaps even cutting, which makes your **2** laugh out loud, but this way of looking a little cynically at the world is not **2**'s preferred approach. They will be grumpy if they think that your fine mind is being wasted on a feeling that it is all hopeless and that nothing can change.

If I am making this all sound negative, that is unfair, for there are many wonderful things that may emerge in this relationship, depending on how many negative characteristics have taken root in each of you. **7**'s positive attributes sit well with **2**'s – an interest in metaphysical or occult thinking, and a high regard for spiritual rather than material truths. Plus, if the **2** is fairly self-confident and feels optimistic about the life you have brought into being around you both, they may be just the person who can co-operate with you, and allow you the time you need to meditate on what is important, and to devise a way of existing with grace in the world you find yourselves in together.

This partnership works best if the female is the **2**, as **7** is truly in awe of **2**'s femininity. Equally, if **7** is forced to take a protective role with **2**, it may bring out your strengths. And it all works a lot better if the **2** is an **11**. But even then, friendship or a mad fling might be better than an expectation of a really long-lasting bond, because 2s will always want more diverse company and fun than 7s, who can be very set in a pattern of privacy and retreat inside their mind too often. Plus, 7 is irritated by 2's frequent forays into mothering the world! And, strangely enough, 7 can be more practical than 2 – although no one may see it that way.

For this to work long-term, much negotiation between differing needs and underlying world views has to be achieved. Perhaps, if you want to badly enough, you will find a way to do just that.

Key themes

Shared quiet time, but sometimes emotions aren't properly expressed • Respect for each other's intelligence; 2 looks up to 7 for their excellent mind • 7 prefers few friends of high calibre, while 2 gets on with most people

6 5 4 3 2 1 9 8 7

7 in love with a 3   ★★★

The one way that this relationship might work is if **3** agrees to be guided by **7**'s higher concentration span. You both have very agile minds, though you like to focus on one thing to the exclusion of others until results come, while **3** dips and dives like a swallow into any number of interesting pursuits – not always bothering to achieve anything substantial. The chase is everything for **3**, but **7** can't tolerate such an inept use of intelligence. Maybe you will encourage **3** to keep focused until they see their ideas through to a conclusion?

But, of course, this is important for a love relationship only if it is going to last, and not all relationships are about that. From the point of view of sheer attraction, the **7** is attracted to the **3** for their undoubted glamour and funny lines, while **3** admires a **7**'s skill in just about everything. **3** almost looks up to **7** – but this is not to say that **3** would like to *be* **7**. You are two different people – marvellous tennis players with very contrasting (and not necessarily well-suited) styles. **3** zips and splashes over a fast grass court with dashing footwork, whereas **7** out-thinks their opponent on a clay court by manoeuvring them into submission, taking much longer to gain the prize. **7** has more reliability in all things, but **3** finds this frustrating after the initial gloss has worn off. Besides, from gregarious **3**'s viewpoint, that strange **7** is always wanting to go off in solitude somewhere, while **3** has the telephone under their chin – and is chatting online at the same time. Little agreement on the social mores of the relationship will also cause combat.

Plus, **7**'s motto of 'still waters run deep' won't necessarily appease **3**'s 'need to know' on most daily things. **3** is used to sharing and bouncing ideas off others, growing in the process and developing newer and even fresher ideas over time. **7** is too wise to give away their own thoughts to others like this, and also very mystical, whereas **3** is canny and sharp. Of course, this could be a wonderful marriage of opposites, so that **3** gains, in the **7**'s higher interests, an outlet for their own brilliance – you effectively drawing your **3** out, and showing them what they're capable of if they can be decisive and apply their mind to something demanding for longer periods. **3** can be intuitive, and aware instinctively of how people feel and what they need. But **7** will feel like darkness and light to sunny **3**, and however much attraction there is some of the time, for a serious relationship there are bound to be difficulties.

Sharing a common number would help hugely – if either of you has a common LIFE number, for instance (*see page 214*). Also, if you have the letters C, L or U in your name, you will have a greater tolerance for **3**'s restlessness and dramatic flair. Essentially, however, this is a relationship that would demand greater compromise than either of you probably wants to make. Enjoy it as a fling, but be ready to move on when the urge takes you! **7** never takes **3** seriously, and never seems to laugh except ironically – perhaps more than **3** can handle?

Key themes

Excellent minds of different ilk • Emotional needs not addressed • Respect for each other's differences (but problems because of them) • Better as business partnership, as can borrow from each other's contrasting talents

7 in love with a 4   ★★★★★

This relationship has a natural order, with **7** behaving as the serious thinker, and **4** the doer; but this works extremely well. **4** is comparatively lacklustre around noble-minded **7**, but again this works to your advantage. So often **7**s are hampered by having brilliant ideas and no method, but **4** is the remedy, scything through your more impractical side and refusing to allow you to be so self-indulgent. **7**'s worst flaw, perhaps, is to be overly aware of their own problems, and not nearly aware enough of other people's, but **4** will point this out in blunt language and prevent the otherwise gifted **7** from wallowing too much – an excellent thing!

4's gritty determination to get things done and to survive hardships is just what you need. So much intellect and such a sharp wit can be self-defeating, if it seems as though there is no point in voicing criticism or acting upon an idea just because it is likely to fall on deaf ears. Such is **7**'s malaise. **4** won't have a bar of this: where there's a will there's a way, and they will put your exceptional observations and analysis into a practical enough gear to make things happen. Together, you have the resolve to achieve much that is for the betterment of those around you.

Each is drawn to the other's apparent self-sufficiency and slight intellectual arrogance towards other more undisciplined numbers. **4** is resentful and disparaging about those who seem to make it in the world without any real intelligence or proper talent; and **7** is simply cynical about this. **4** brings a serious talent for practical planning and organization to the imaginative and insightful **7**, and you lift each other to greater heights as a result. You inspire **4** to take their knowledge and skill to another level, while they encourage you to leave behind past disappointments, and make a start in the here-and-now. It's a good balance.

7 is always enigmatic and interesting – which intrigues

4. Your plane of existence is so cerebral that you need a down-to-earth person to help you achieve. **7**s are so often despairing of what the world is experiencing, while **4**s find comfort where it can be found – digging in the garden, offering reliable friendship to a close group, keeping personal affairs in order. **7** needs this desperately. And you are so charming and funny that **4** can't help offering unequivocal admiration for this. Your aptitude for repartee and pithy summations will provoke **4** to articulate their own verbal gems – so often lost under a cloud of insecurity. Literally, **4** is enriched by **7**'s talents and accomplishments.

And there is a chemistry at work here. You are amused by **4**'s no-nonsense attitude, which accords well with your ironic take on things. **7** is often such a loner, because no one seems worth the trouble of explaining the complexities of life to; but **4** is a good listener, and suddenly you have a companion who recognizes your exceptional insight. Though you are such a perfectionist, which **4** respects, **4** understands that many things in life can't always *be* perfect, and persuades you to be content sometimes with the best that can be done in the circumstances. And you lift **4**'s attention to a more spiritual and humanitarian dimension, showing them colours they never guessed were in the spectrum.

4 needs to be forgiving of the shadows that lurk from **7**'s past: a **7** is who and what they are as a result of turning past experience into philosophical thought. That may never quite go away. But **4** will be excited by your superior poise and dignity — like their uprightness, but differently expressed. This partnership is one of the best that can be.

Key themes

Common ground over social concerns • Both very intelligent • **4** the doer, **7** the architect • **4** makes **7** more sanguine, **7** lifts **4**'s thoughts up to a more philosophical and spiritual level • Enjoy time alone together

---

6   5   4   3   2   1   9   8   7

7 in love with a 5   ★★★

We could say that opposites attract ... or is this really more about the challenge factor? Here, we have the naturally exuberant, freedom-loving, sexually demanding and adventurous **5**, fascinated and in love with the high-minded, intelligent, ever-challenging yet reserved **7**. The **5**, on one hand, is physical, materialistic, progressive, with keen intelligence and a quick grasp of most things, while the **7**, on the other, is spiritual, analytical, cerebral, contemplative and a seeker of wisdom and truth.

There is no doubt that this relationship will stimulate you both for entirely different reasons, bursting with creative and inspirational discussions, evenings out, tête-à-têtes when you can have your sexy **5** to yourself, or, at the end of a dinner party, when you find yourselves alone and in front of a crackling fire. I doubt that you were at the

| 7 | 8 | 9 | 1 | 2 | 3 | 4 | 5 | 6 |

party the night before, though, because **7** doesn't favour those packed venues or mindless banter. This is a marriage of truly curious and inquisitive minds, in a way. Your enigmatic reserve and intelligence are a magnet for **5**, who seems to reach into their most spiritual inclinations when they come together with your number, because **7** is capable of such depth, and **5** is – while bright and vivacious – more of a rocket on the way to Mars.

Yours is a very private number, and things will teeter if your entrancing **5** is in any way indiscriminate. Also, if they are too demanding (sexually or in their desire for answers about your life), they will lose you: **7**s insist on keeping some corners of their personality away from everybody else – even from the love of their life. This will be a challenge every day – and in most situations where **5**'s affable and curious personality bounces in where angels fear to tread. Although **5**s are warm, unprejudiced and skilful in finding things out, even they may feel that there is a darker truth behind your surface – experiences or loneliness that might explain that complexity and enigmatic depth. **5** may never be allowed to go there, and huge problems will come if they attempt to blast their way through this reserve, for they must try to allow your love affair time. You will say whatever you are going to say to your own agenda – and pushing will alienate you both.

5 is an extroverted introvert, while you are a little bit introverted – at least in some departments. Family memories and early shaping experiences cast a long shadow. You need your lover to be aware of your need for truth and honesty, but also your desire for independence. If a relationship between you is to work, you will have to cultivate more patience than you usually show towards each other, and signal to your exuberant **5** not to be too 'dark' in bed.

They must try to accept your healthy lifestyle/cleanliness fetish – at odds with their own relaxed attitude. **7** thrives in an environment that is elegant and precise, while

5 is in need of 'help' in most areas on the home front, as far as organization and method is concerned. Call in the professional services that you can afford, to keep things running (and the home clean and clear of clutter!). More than any other number, **5** needs 'gentle organizers' – someone to come regularly to clean and mend, and help put things into order, or a personal assistant who will co-ordinate as an 'angel' working the necessary miracles. You will never scold your **5** about the budget for such necessities!

Key themes

5 strains against 7's perfectionism, privacy requirements, solitude, and obsessive and meticulous demands • Expect a push/pull scenario, but shared communication and personal sensitivity will help!

---

7 in love with a 6 ★

Your two numbers are going to be at sixes and sevens, of course! (It's interesting to ponder where this expression comes from: it is certainly clear in its meaning of confusion.) **7** has a feeling of intellectual arrogance and a disinterest in banality – which is fair enough, given your delicate sensibility and lack of patience for the public taste. **6** finds this exclusiveness interesting and even attractive, but ultimately restricting. Put simply, **6** gets on with everyone, and is interested in diversity and popular culture, whereas **7** is frustrated by this apparent lack of discrimination.

This isn't a problem initially: **6** sees fascinating **7**, who looks like they need a patient listener and a good-hearted person to discover their pain and enigmatic personality. You enjoy food together, and though you have different styles and tastes you are perfectly capable of extending each other's experience. **6** seems so genuinely peaceable and laissez-faire about the world, attractive and arts-minded, and disinclined to be jealous of others' success or lucky breaks: surely all guaranteed to pique **7**'s interest, for it is so different from the way a **7** responds? And isn't **6** appreciative of **7**'s mind and sharp humour, and **7** admiring of **6**'s aesthetic taste and good looks? Indeed it is so; but after an initial enthralment, the reality of being quite disparate people starts to flavour the relationship, and it all may go sour.

A **6** will look up to your intelligence and even your aristocratic taste and bearing; and you admire all that is fluid and generous in **6**, for you are naturally critical and even self-castigating at times. But this critical factor is part of what disenchants your **6** over time, because they are forgiving and wise in giving everyone a chance to show themselves in their best light, whereas you like birds of a feather, and are a specialist and a perfectionist: too fussy, perhaps, for easy **6**, not nearly relaxed enough for them, and very demanding around the home – even in a **6**'s eyes!

Still waters run deep, and **6** has an idea that you have a captivating personal tale to tell. Quite right: but you won't always want to share, or draw a line on the past, or explain a dark mood that momentarily descends. **6** respects your wish for peace, but eventually begins to feel walled out. And, as much as **6** wants a beautiful shared space to live in, you may be a bit obsessive for their taste. When **6** wants a glass of wine at the end of the day, a **7** – depending on mood – will either join in too heartily or be on a detox diet, and force everyone else to accept their opinions on health and lifestyle. **6** puts finishing touches to the bathroom with a pretty bunch of scented flowers, but you wonder why they're not white, like the liquid soap and hand towels. You demand such attention to detail, while **6** feels life's too short to be so compulsive. And if you feel a little negative or uninspired, or have had a broken heart once too often, **6** will feel all alone in this relationship.

| 7 | 8 | 9 | 1 | 2 | 3 | 4 | 5 | 6 |

Occasionally this pairing works better than its one-star rating – if you have learned from experience to relax a little, and to appreciate what is different in taste from your own inclinations, and if the **6** has achieved self-discipline and maturity about love relationships, and doesn't feel the need to be constantly reassured by your words of love (which are often not forthcoming). You don't always notice how controlling you can be, nor how unintentionally brusque. It will depend on how flexible and good-humoured **6** is as to how seriously any slights are felt. Be very wise with each other!

Key themes

Both arts-lovers who enjoy a cultured life and friends coming by, but **7** needs far more privacy and discerning company • Problems arise if **6** needs emotional reassurances, or if **7** is hyper-critical and controlling

| 6 | 5 | 4 | 3 | 2 | 1 | 9 | 8 | 7 |

7 in love with a 7 ★★★

There is a physical pull between two **7**s – an actual, real sexual magnetism. This is down to the thrilling, sensual mind games that go on between two people excited by qualities of intelligence and perception so like their own in another human being. Two **7**s have so much in common: similar discriminatory tastes; a love of getting something exactly right – be it a weekend break or plans for a home extension; a yearning to expand their knowledge throughout their relationship, never atrophying or becoming worn out in their interaction with culture and thought. So why does this pairing only get a three-star rating?

7s together are a mixture of mutual spiritual enlightenment and highly strung intellectual and emotional nervousness. They may bring out the best in each other, in that need to have a little space without retreating into too much damaging isolation; but they may also compete with one another, and turn highly critical when there is emotional pressure or a difference of opinion. It needs to be handled with care.

The best offering between two **7**s may be that they can find peace together. As long as both partners are experienced in the heartbreaks and let-downs of life, as well as mature about what is required to live life at the top, there should be little argument between you and a good understanding of each other's reciprocal needs. This depends on both partners having grown-up emotions, and this is a strong possibility, because **7** thinks long and hard about what has gone amiss before, focusing to overcome setbacks and find personal philosophical enlightenment. When shared with another **7**, this can be extremely satisfying and enriching. Of course, you may both live in rather a cerebral world, and rest aloof (by choice) from the hurdy-gurdy of modern life. This may not seem a practical arrangement to many friends, who will see you as cocooned and unconcerned with the transitory elements of the more material world; but this does not mean you are wrong to find such an earthly haven together.

One potential problem, though, is that the partnership between two 7s can become just too idealized and not grounded enough in the real world, so that your individual talents for reform and the teaching and counselling of others are unused. Always given to a meditational state of mind, two 7s may dwell entirely inside their heads and, to a certain extent, miss the pleasure of the sensory world. This may not seem a sacrifice until it is too late to change, when the chance of children or some degree of material success is passed. There is always a balance to be found between 7's drive to be spiritual and not fall into the trap of meaningless consumerism, and their failure to actuate their talents for the good of the wider community. 7s sometimes languish a little, and feel personal disappointment and even failure later in life: nothing, perhaps, may contribute to this more than a relationship with another **7**, who is equally unconcerned in addressing problems and turning life into achievements.

But if this does not matter to you, it may be that three stars are inadequate to describe the nirvana that two truly philosophical thinkers – who may be mature and selfless to a great degree – can find. Just try to recruit a house-keeper or a private secretary who can pay the bills and weed the garden, or remind you if a deadline looms on the work front!

Key themes

Understated sexual magnetism • Meeting of like minds • Danger of competition with one another • May be too cerebral and not grounded enough • Can work well if both partners are emotionally mature

| 6 | 5 | 4 | 3 | 2 | 1 | 9 | 8 | 7 |

7 in love with an 8 ★★★★

8 will entice **7**. Different and yet similar in fascinating ways, the difficulties that come from a joining of two **7**s – who are loath to balance the material requirements of the world with their own personal priorities – melt away with this partnership. **8** has the ambition **7** often lacks, and yet also offers **7**'s meditative mind some further food for thought.

Anyone involved with an **8** will come to learn that they are doers, power-walkers, thrill-seekers. If something cannot be done in theory, **8** wants to disprove that. Such a viewpoint fascinates you, as you love a challenge just from the intellectual standpoint, and, as a pair, you extend each other's vision and sense of possibility. **8** often bluffs through impossible situations, but intelligent **7** shows **8** a little refinement, and that achievements can still be perfected. This offers a heightened physical attraction and –

| 7 | 8 | 9 | 1 | 2 | 3 | 4 | 5 | 6 |

ultimately — the chance for real love to blossom.

8 has much productive fire in their soul, and this may occasionally overwhelm you; but your **8** lover also has what it takes to fire you up — out of intellectual malaise or physical lethargy — into an inspirational mental space. You have such vision and inner poise, and this in turn challenges **8** to find a subject worthy of your combined energies — be it in humanitarian enterprises, successful productive business, or in areas of research and academia which forge new understanding and awareness. This can lift you into a higher gear, where your adrenaline rush is exciting and stimulating. In other words, **8**'s forceful nature galvanizes **7** into astonishing artistic or intellectual output, and the love develops along the way.

For **8** — who has a fine mind like **7** — you are someone to organize. They see your sensitivity and perceptive powers, and are strongly attracted to that natural hauteur which sets you apart from the crowd — and they love it. **8**s are only ever excited by quality – never by quantity. Their own cast of mind is philosophical, and looks at both sides of an argument or situation, and your **8** lover's mind will be busy and stocked with varying interests which are guaranteed to intrigue you. The good thing is that, as a **7**, you have the calming personality to make the **8** slow down a little. **8** is a strenuous number, demanding a great deal from the holder; and perhaps only **7** in the wide world has the perceptual power and wisdom to prevent this intriguing, charismatic human being from reaching burn-out. With an **8** you will feel needed – though occasionally you will lust for some stillness.

In a nutshell, this is a potential mutual love affair. **8** must not be too controlling, and must allow **7** to go at its own pace; but your **8** lover has just the strength you need to draw on in crisis moments, and **7**'s rationalizing and serene intellectual grasp of all situations can direct **8**'s daring and brilliant mind to the best prize for both of you.

| 7 | 8 | 9 | 1 | 2 | 3 | 4 | 5 | 6 |

Key themes

7 channels 8's energies into august projects and
inspirational interests • 8 is the strong guide-rail for 7 to
hold on to in a downpour • 8 attracts important people,
while 7's nobility of character takes both partners to a
special plateau of thought and achievement • Strong love

7 in love with a 9   ★★★

Boasting a tremendous charm, and a rich imagination and appreciation of arts and ideas, **9** strongly appeals to **7**. Together you have a powerful sympathy and feeling for other people, but **9** is also a good companion and a fun-loving yet intelligent friend, and this is important to a **7**. **9** may be able to make you laugh when no one else can, being a natural actor and having a good, facile mind; you sometimes needs to be chivvied out of too much self-analysis, and **9** can do this. You will be drawn to a **9** lover, in fact, largely because they are willing and able to stand up to you. **7** can be so high-handed with other mortal thinkers, often unintentionally, but **9** won't stand for this arrogance — and won't take offence, either. And this is excellent medicine for **7**.

A **9** can also share deeply probing conversations with

| 7 | 8 | 9 | 1 | 2 | 3 | 4 | 5 | 6 |

you, as you each have a love of literature and good expression, of film, and of the arts generally. **9** will approve of your discerning mind, and when we speak of **7** having a 'desert island' mentality, where only a privileged few may be invited, **9** is certainly one of those guests with a pass to virtually all areas. **9** even exceeds **7**'s distaste for small-minded and over-materialistic people and situations, and you two may be witty critics of cultural faux pas together.

So, again, why only three stars? Part of the problem is that **9** can be very idealistic and a bit over-indulgent about their personal life and emotional stresses. **7** expects more grown-up behaviour, not prone personally to bleeding publicly if there is a problem. And **9** may possibly fall in love with a little too much gusto for a **7**'s taste: you are always excited by the understated, the enigmatic, the hard-to-get. Both of you are dreamers, but a **9**'s dreams are based on idealism and a **7**'s on spirituality. There is excellent ground between you two for friendship and a positive love affair, but promises of the great hereafter may not suit, for you are ultimately going in different directions.

Once the sexual attraction quietens, you will become frustrated with **9**, who is a jack of many trades but rarely quite enough of a master of any of them to the satisfaction of fussy, perfectionist **7**. This may seem a small and even amusing warning, but over time it will grate. **9**s don't like being goaded too far, or asked to gift their good grace indefinitely without something in return. Though genuinely in awe of your poise and personal dignity, it fears clever **7** can also be too selfish — and there is some justice in this. **9** is a big brother to the world, where **7** is proud and a little reserved. These essential characteristics can lead to difficulties in the everyday mechanics of the relationship.

What definitely works is the high intelligence and respect for bigger ideas you each have, and this includes a thrill you get from reading and talking deeply, pondering the best way to achieve joy and social justice. What is not so good is the fact that **9** is an endearing grown-up child, full of enthusiasm and responsive emotions, whereas **7** is a born parent, middle-aged at five! Sympathies exist between you, and your hearts and souls are in the right place. If the mystical elements in your personalities are dominant, then the three-star rating may seem a little mean. The bond is better if you are older, perhaps.

Key themes

Shared depth of feeling and hopes of harmony for the world and its people, but **9** more people-orientated than **7** · **7** wishes **9** would be less like a bouncing puppy occasionally, while **9** would like **7** to loosen up!

6   5   4   3   2   1   9   8   7

7 in love with an 11   ★★★★

We have already looked at your relationship with a pure **2** (*see page 140*), but what does it mean if the **2** happens to also be master number **11** (born on the 11th or 29th of the month)? Is this likely to improve things, or make them worse? The master numbers have a different impact on relationships – and it is definitely one to appeal to the finer mind and discriminatory powers of an intelligent **7** ...

And, in this case, the **7/11** combination definitely has much greater potential for success than the straight **7/2** pairing. If you are involved with an **11**, this can truly be an excellent partnership. You so often build that protective coating around you in relationships, and highly instinctive **11** is also a bit of a loner, and will respect this need for privacy in you. You are both verbal chess-players, and it will be interesting – and perhaps even genuinely entertaining for both of you — to see how you fence words together and come to a deeper understanding of your individual selves. You may be able to lift the sometimes over-committed **11** out of the rapid water so that they can actually see where they are going: this is a great service to them, for **11**s are immensely talented and often just need directing.

Both **7** and **11** are prime numbers — and you are prime people. You share that little bit of arrogance — not always a bad thing — and you can each be dignified and gracious with others, good company, quick-witted, and admired for your grasp of situations and events. You also both have a social conscience, and a relationship between you might well be derived from working in a common organization where you are thrown together with distinctive but complementary talents to achieve some mastery. This you can do. You are attracted to this individual, who is absolutely an individual — and, having matched minds as to expectation of others and unshrinking self-criticism, you may together achieve quite extraordinary heights and a great deal of personal development.

And perhaps it is good that you are capable of telling your fascinating **11** lover when they are being just too impractical. Someone has to. The infuriating thing for you about your **11** is that they are clearly so able, so clever, and particularly inspirational to other people; yet they live by rules all their own, sometimes refusing to see the writing when it is irrefutably vivid on the wall. This can be exhilarating, watching someone refuse to accept limitations. But it can also be heartbreaking, and occasionally you will have to take control and be a little brutal.

Together, you have a sophistication, a mutual appetite for more knowledge and an apprehension of the world in its intellectual, emotional and mystical realms. If you work with each other, you can build great bridges over rough terrain.

Key themes

Thrill at certain similarities of character, but **7** needs to manoeuvre **11** out of the dangerous zones into spheres of potential joy and tolerance for others • Possibly a highly metaphysical relationship

7 in love with a 22   ★★★★★

Like an **11**, someone born on the 22nd of the month seems to sizzle with cool potential and the promise of escaping a jejune life at any level. **22** also makes things happen, and lures you to admire their superior intelligence and outstanding people skills. Something about a **22** is riveting to you: they look, sound and act differently from every other human being. But they can be just as determined and non-compliant with fools and gullible people as you can. You will certainly share only a very select and worthy band of close friends, and you will look down on much that is considered 'successful' if it lacks any substance in the popular world. A **7** and a **22** cuddling up in front of a soap opera can hardly be imagined!

Nor will **22** put up with your retirement from the world, because your attractively bossy **22** lover sees you as

| 7 | 8 | 9 | 1 | 2 | 3 | 4 | 5 | 6 |

a unique potential contributor to the better ideas and understanding of other people. They will push you to write that novel or paint that picture, or get that film funded or finish that PhD. **22** won't let you slide into oblivion. And you may also contribute to your **22**'s success, understanding precisely what is required from others to support their inspirational plans. **22** is the master builder in numerology, and **7** is very much an architectural thinker – almost an architect of the mind. That is one reason why this relationship between you can work at such a high level.

What is happening with the number **22** is that we are dealing with the repetition of the highly spiritual and feminized **2**, which is effectively doubling the sensation of Light – light being a spiritual beacon. For you, as a **7**, this is intensely appealing. A **22** will strike you as a soul apart – just as you so often appear to others. But in relationships there can be tensions in a **22** that will make some days or heavy weather between you. This is because they can feel conflict over personal desires and social duties. If you love a **22**, remember that they can feel strange inner cravings for affection — like a **2** — even though they are so seemingly self-sufficient and confident. Your **22** lover needs your help and support desperately, because they have important work to do. If they are not expressing this heightened talent in a realized way, they are not yet being true to themselves, and it may be that you are the one who can help them find their real pleasure in this life — which is partly to help others on a large scale.

A **22** will make you try hard, laugh loud, cry at times in fellow-feeling, and maybe sometimes you will need to look them in the eye and bring them back down to earth, or offer them some serenity and cooling time. But this you can live with. **22**'s inspirational aura blended with personal practicality may suit your nobility of nature and high intelligence very well. This is why it is a five-star tie — for a **22** will be like no one else you have dated!

| 7 | 8 | 9 | 1 | 2 | 3 | 4 | 5 | 6 |

Key themes

Both have brilliant minds and must analyse and build something in this world at the political or scientific level • **22** is very secure and will make **7** feel appreciated • Happiness depends on mutual goals

Work

YOUR **WORK** COMPATIBILITY CHART

	1	2	3	4	5
With a 1	★★★★	★★★★★	★	★★★	★★★
With a 2	★★★★★	★★★	★★★	★★★★	★
With a 3	★	★★★	★★★★	★★	★★★★★
With a 4	★★★	★★★★	★★	★★★★★	★★★
With a 5	★★★	★	★★★★★	★★★	★★
With a 6	★★	★★★★★	★★★★	★★★★	★★★★
With a 7	★★★★★	★★★	★★★	★★★★★	★★
With an 8	★★★★★	★★★★★	★★★★★	★★★	★★★★
With a 9	★★★★	★★★	★★★★★	★★	★★★
With an 11	★★	★★★★	★★★	★★★★★	★★
With a 22	★★★★★	★★	★★★	★★★	★★★★

7   8   9   1   2   3   4   5   6

6	7	8	9	11	22
★★	★★★★★	★★★★★	★★★★	★★	★★★★★
★★★★★	★★★	★★★★★	★★★	★★★★	★★
★★★★	★★★	★★★★★	★★★★★	★★★	★★★
★★★★	★★★★★	★★★	★★	★★★★★	★★★
★★★★	★★	★★★★	★★★	★★	★★★★
★★★	★	★★★★	★★★	★★★★★	★★★★
★	★★★★	★★★	★★	★★★★	★★★★★
★★★★	★★★	★★★	★★★★	★★★★★	★★★★
★★★	★★	★★★★	★★★	★★★★★	★★★★★
★★★★★	★★★★	★★★★★	★★★★★	★★★★	★★★★★
★★★★	★★★★★	★★★★	★★★★★	★★★★★	★★★

6 5 4 3 2 1 9 8 7

7 working with a 1   ★★★★★

You two make a very positive pairing in business. You are both full of inner strength, and like to do things brilliantly, never settling for second best. In fact, you can perfect what **1** starts, and you are able to retire to opposite sides of a room and get on with it, without interference. You may have the specialist education that a **1** admires, where they have the raw ability and daring you may feel you lack. **1**'s fearlessness combined with **7**'s discipline could move financial mountains, so suffice to say you're a good team.

Your working options together are unlimited, because **7** is brilliant at research and **1** is a pioneer/explorer type. You will find interesting ways of looking at problems, and spur each other to solve them together; but where **1** can be something of a jack of all trades, you like to specialize – which they value. **1** asks a question, and you will know how and where to find the answer.

You're both quick on the uptake, and neither of you needs another person to agree with what you envisage. You are replete as a band of two, and many new frontiers at work have been achieved through this kind of partnership. You would be happiest in your own shared business, rather than working for a corporation, but as long as you have a degree of autonomy you will succeed very well together at almost anything you try. You'll be especially in your element if you can find a work environment that offers rural tranquillity – even if it is in the city – or if the building you occupy is unusual. In an ideal world, **1** and **7** will gravitate towards water, or a park, for an office location!

Key themes

Well suited for team work • Good grasp of one another's strengths • Respect for each other's minds

6   5   4   3   2   1   9   8   7

7 working with a 2   ★★★

This relationship works very well in specialist areas, as this brings out the best in **7**, and **2** will be a detailed and organized helpmate. You love to hone your mind on what is difficult to perfect – taking up challenges no one else wants to touch. **2** is a wonderful support here, because both numbers succeed well in research areas, and don't need a party atmosphere to feel work is rewarding. Your goals are similar, and you share a love of a job really well done. Plus, **2** has great admiration for your intelligence and inner stillness.

More than this, **2** can deflect public attention or distracting liaisons away from you when you have your head down. **7**'s challenge is to get on with the job and produce something as perfect as possible, without having to explain intentions to outside parties. **2** realizes this, and wants to protect you from irritations that slow up the process.

| 7 | 8 | 9 | 1 | 2 | 3 | 4 | 5 | 6 |

Things can go sour if you are arrogant – which sometimes happens! – so that the **2** feels patronized or overlooked. **2** always has contributions to make that are worth
hearing; but sometimes **7**s become so fixated on their own
plans that there is little consultation with others, and **2**
becomes aggrieved by this neglect. The other problem is
that you often take your personal woes out on others without meaning to, but never offer an explanation or apology.
Intuitive **2** will realize this is the case, but may feel indig-
nation that you are unable to be honest about this simple
thing with others – to the potential detriment of group
harmony. Overall, though, the energy between **2** and **7** in
the workplace is good and produces excellent results.

Key themes

Innate understanding · Mutual respect · Attention to detail
· Research work ideal

| 6 | 5 | 4 | 3 | 2 | 1 | 9 | 8 | 7 |

7 working with a 3   ★★★

When you give each other room to function smoothly, this work relationship may be better than its three-star rating might suggest. **3** can appreciate your skills and ability to specialize in one field, knowing everything about it. This is not the way a **3** does things, but they recognize that somebody should. What will bother them is if you seem a little arrogant or high-handed about your own contributions.

In fact, **7** can frustrate **3** at work, because your very clever humour is often biting and negative, and your tongue often critical and shrewd. **3** would rather find a solution to personnel problems than simply identify them, and may feel that you are caught up in your own space, own world, own interests. It is true that a **7** in the office can seem selfish – but if you trust the **3** and let them gently bring this to your attention, you are astonishingly gracious and willing to modify your direction. As a **7**, you may sometimes be blinkered, but neither cruel nor unconcerned with other people's needs.

3's talent is to dip and dive and hustle – which **7** can appreciate, but wouldn't want to replicate. This is a work tie that demands – and usually achieves – mutual respect and a little room for manoeuvre. **7** is best left to get on with things, and a **3** may not always understand how or why you do things as you do; but they will trust your intentions and appreciate the results you get. Just ask them not to use your personal coffee mug without checking with you first!

Key themes

Different approaches (flamboyant/dignified) bring interesting results • Respect for each other essential

6   5   4   3   2   1   9   8   **7**

7 working with a 4   ★★★★★

It shouldn't take much imagination to see that this has real potential. Built on mutual respect and a willingness to overlook the more intractable areas in each other's work personalities, **4** understands **7**'s need for clean, airy peace and calm and a quiet place to think, while recognizing that superior ideas are born in this superior mind. And, in return, **7** appreciates **4**'s willingness to provide exactly the right atmosphere and furnish the precise kind of data that is required to determine how to tackle a business demand. These numbers fill in around each other, without having to consult as to what is missing or required.

    7 seems to have a sixth sense, as far as **4** is concerned, seeing (accurately) what will appeal to the most diverse group of people, and possessing the right attitude towards marketing to make a success out of a clever venture. Yet

| 7 | 8 | 9 | 1 | 2 | 3 | 4 | 5 | 6 |

you can also be forgetful, or have a selective memory about what you have agreed or thought. Here, **4** rescues the missing information, and brings you – so often on a lofty plateau – down to earth just long enough to achieve the goal needed. And you come to appreciate **4** for this feat. This pairing is a blend of architect and builder – the one wholly dependent on the skills of the other – and it works.

4 will often think **7** too cerebral, and **7** may bemoan **4**'s cautiousness or lack of vision; but these perceptions will be made and stated without malice. Seeing what is – and what isn't – there, the two numbers find an excellent system for functioning at the highest level, and would make superb partners in their own business.

Key themes

4 examines the ground for an understanding of the terrain, while **7** scans the skies for signs of inspiration. Poetry!

| 6 | 5 | 4 | 3 | 2 | 1 | 9 | 8 | 7 |

7 working with a 5   ★★

This is a little like the coming together of the jazz band and the classical trio! While there is little doubting your individual talents, they are diametrically opposed. 5s are quick on the uptake, skilful, productive and progressive, while 7s are analytical specialists, refined, logical, accurate and erudite. 7 may not be convinced by 5's dilettantism, distracted by the scattering force of their multi-faceted energy.

At times, you can perfect what 5 creates, and you may retire to opposite sides of a room and get on without interference. You may have the specialist education that 5 admires, where they have the raw dynamic sales ability and daring you may feel you lack. 5's free thinking joined to 7's discipline could move financial mountains, so suffice to say this union can create material satisfaction for each of you and, in this way, you can become a good team.

| 7 | 8 | 9 | 1 | 2 | 3 | 4 | 5 | 6 |

One of the problems is that you are discerning in your outlook, selecting projects you can interest yourself with. **5** is always more radical, alive to a wider group of people, keen to try something risky, where a **7** shrugs and wonders about the waste of time. You're watching the horizon for charlatans, while **5** is beguiled and excited by the pirates and the pioneers! And, somehow, this difference grates.

Individual autonomy will help you to function simultaneously; thus you would be happiest in your own shared business, rather than working for a corporation. Potential disasters relate to **5**'s mode of attack: you may bristle at their ill-timed flamboyance and the disarray they leave in their wake. You need a tranquil space for this to succeed.

Key themes

5 produces ideas, **7** refines them · Need to understand each other's weaknesses · **7** offended by **5**'s disregard for accuracy

| 6 | 5 | 4 | 3 | 2 | 1 | 9 | 8 | 7 |

7 working with a 6   ★

Hmmn ... not sure about this one. Your different styles — which can be entertaining in love relationships — could really lead to clashes or suppressed feelings. **6** so rarely lets fly when there is a hurt or slight, preferring to keep everything (and everybody) cheerful; but **7** can't help being biting and critical if anyone is shirking their load. The **6** will laugh out loud sometimes — because your tongue is razor-sharp and very funny; but this is not how they do business. Where **6** wants to offer someone a chance to get started, you doubt they will maximize their chance (possibly only too correctly!), and there will be fallout if you are right.

6 also undermines **7**'s strategies occasionally, being too causal in their opinion about the way things should be done, or relying too heavily on charm and surface impressions and not seeing deeply into things and people. **6** gives everyone the benefit of the doubt, and **7**, almost no one! Plus **7** is a specialist who likes to work with other perfectionist/specialists, whereas **6** is so capable of dipping into many requirements. You won't trust **6**'s jack-of-all-trades ability, and may miss out on something very special in their talents by refusing to take them seriously.

You appreciate **6**'s artistic touch and understanding of what will be popular in the marketplace, and they admire your focus and determination to know the whole of any subject. Thus, at best, this may become a marriage of opposites which works well enough, if you give each other space and respect to do things differently. But, methinks, it is walking on eggshells for each of you.

Key themes

6 flatters **7**'s ego but only briefly, finding **7** too sharp · Good intelligence, but clashing styles with potential flare-ups

6	5	4	3	2	1	9	8	7

7 working with a 7   ★★★★

This business relationship has surprising fire and energy. The two of you are lit with a powerful inner imagination and a credo that demands working to the highest level of perfection possible. Wishing to extend accepted territories by breaking into uncharted ground, you are perhaps not so much pioneers as visionaries, who can see what will make a better product/idea/service than what went before.

Another **7** will have a good understanding of how you feel under pressure and will leave you well enough alone, accepting that you rarely – if ever – let the side down, and that you must be left to your own devices, unwatched, if you are to perform. You will also get a good deal of productive criticism from another **7**, who will appreciate your sensitivity to being told anything isn't perfect, while also realizing that you will be driven to get it better, to perfect.

| 7 | 8 | 9 | 1 | 2 | 3 | 4 | 5 | 6 |

Honesty won't come between you.

As partners, your intuition matches up well, and your ability to see around corners may seem uncanny. It is important, though, that you specialize in differing areas so that you complement rather than contradict one another. 7s – all of them – have strong opinions. But the office atmosphere should be quite serene and the building beautiful enough with your combined good taste. Overall, excellent!

Key themes

Work towards perfection · Understand each other's sensitivities · Need complementary specialist areas if to achieve the best results · Afford each other privacy

6   5   4   3   2   1   9   8   7

7 working with an 8   ★★★

Though these two numbers spark off each other very well in a personal relationship, they are — surprisingly — not so well suited in business. Such different methods are attractive in a personal bond, but in the boardroom **7** is frightened at times by **8**'s approach, and **8** is disappointed at clever **7**'s lack of acumen about money. Not that **7** is foolish around finances, but **8** will always need a reliable, up-front partner who is as courageous and flamboyant as they are. **8** sees endless possibilities, while **7** is not so driven by the material world. Day to day, as friends or lovers, this isn't a problem: in fact, **8**'s attention to financial requirements gives **7** the freedom not to be so fettered. But, in a work relationship, this becomes a frustration for both of you.

From the practical, material point of view, an **8** realizes only too well that pragmatism is often necessary in the

| 7 | 8 | 9 | 1 | 2 | 3 | 4 | 5 | 6 |

world of financial reality. Although you have finesse and vision, you are unwilling to bend over backwards for someone you see being dishonest or unscrupulous. **8** can bite their tongue, but **7** cannot. And so the honesty thing becomes a thorn in **8**'s side ... which is not to say that **7**'s moral feelings are not absolutely justified; but **8** sees the need to be a diplomat, to flatter and cajole, whereas this is below **7**'s dignity.

In working life, other people will love or loathe, lionize or lose it with a **7** for their pride and hauteur. An **8** – remaining dignified but flexible – will tear their hair out. So, not impossible, but definitely a high-wire act where both of you must do a lot of balancing!

Key themes

8 may seem too carnivorous about business for herbivorous **7** · Excellent minds, which need room to function

| 6 | 5 | 4 | 3 | 2 | 1 | 9 | 8 | 7 |

7 working with a 9 ★★

This is more likely to stifle each partner's creative and intellectual powers than propel you to business paradise. **9** wants to be in charge of – and try out – many things; this is against your nature, as **7**s become positively scathing about anyone trying their hand if they are not a specialist trained for the job. **9** is just too relaxed with others, and **7** may seem too isolated and content in their own space. While both numbers seek inner truths and personal growth in life generally, you have different ways of attacking this objective. Business-wise, **9** is restless and prefers to travel, while you like to concentrate on achieving the best that can be, and not move on until that has been reached. Plus, you tire of **9**'s emotional life spilling into the office. You keep your emotions on a tight leash; how can **9** be so casual about their intimate life?

| 7 | 8 | 9 | 1 | 2 | 3 | 4 | 5 | 6 |

On the other hand, there is a good meeting of minds if the business direction is artistic or humanitarian in any way – science or medicine, literature or the arts. Then, you may work peaceably, without cut-throat techniques. And your understanding of what makes others work will help immeasurably. Your combined talents could offer a cushion of wisdom for those around you.

Success or failure depends on how much respect you develop for each other, and what field you operate in. **9** admires your mind and self-motivation, but worries about your sharp tongue. If you can find a way past these blocks, there may be something excellent to uncover in a business relationship. But agree to do things very differently.

Key themes

Contrasting styles: **7** a perfectionist, **9** interested in many outlets for their talents • Works best in arts or sciences

6 5 4 3 2 1 9 8 7

7 working with an 11 ★★★★

This works better than with a straight **2**. High ideals and a feeling for what may yet be characterize the overall feeling between your two numbers. In business, an **11** will enthral and intrigue you. There are many disparate factors in an **11**'s personality – their apparent ego and yet a true self-doubt born of the understanding that, clever and alert as they are, they are a long way from being who and what they wish to be. You recognize this trait, as there are corners of it which describe you too. Both of you are independent and somewhat headstrong, but you achieve a firm respect for one another which ameliorates those irritations you cause with your fussiness and extremely high personal standards.

An **11** will speak with magnetism, and if you arrive at a pecking order where one of you takes dominion over

| 7 | 8 | 9 | 1 | 2 | 3 | 4 | 5 | 6 |

the public liaisons (this should probably be the **11**) and the other handles information and research (best if this is you), you will cover a vast amount of territory. Neither an **11** nor a **7** can sit happily with mediocrity. Always gently pushing to reach a more informed state of being, you will lift each other on doldrum days and be sensitive to one another's dreams and despairs. Certainly, no fools will be permitted to work within a mile of either of you, and you will share a wicked but elevating sense of humour.

The best area for expression would be in any public service or entertainments sphere, or in the realms of writing and research. It's hard to envisage an **11/7** partnership being anything less than cutting edge!

Key themes

Acuity in everything: insights, judgement, knowledge base, understanding, intuition

| 6 | 5 | 4 | 3 | 2 | 1 | 9 | 8 | 7 |

7 working with a 22 ★★★★★

22 will hoist you up the mainsail just at the point when the book was getting interesting and the horizon lulling you into calm. No resting on laurels for you if a **22** is around! They have more ambition than you do, which is excellent for business — and yet you still share an implicit need for quiet working conditions, peaceable co-workers, and the agreement that it is perfection or nothing that you're aiming for. This sits well with you, and **22** will be both reliable in the tasks they are set (very little being impossible for them!) and willing to rely entirely on you when it is your turn to shine. This confidence and appreciation you are shown will encourage you to push a little harder at work, and your career may really take off with such a soul near you.

Just as your own work field is unlimited and varied, a

| 7 | 8 | 9 | 1 | 2 | 3 | 4 | 5 | 6 |

22 is suited to many tasks and strengths. You share an excellent head for researching and gathering statistics, for sharp observations and clever analysis, and for intuitive calculations which prove their worth in time. This makes you a good team, and, if you can accept that the **22** is more of a showman, perhaps, than you are, and more driven to outright success, you may find that it suits you to go along for the ride. Certainly, your finances will prosper more around a **22** than with almost any other number. Great for business, then — as long as you can arrange it so that you're the connoisseur and they're the go-getter!

Key themes

Marriage of find minds at work • Similar goals, though **22** more ambitious, and has a positive goading effect on **7**

Friendship

YOUR **FRIENDSHIP** COMPATIBILITY CHART

	1	2	3	4	5
With a 1	★★★	★★★★★	★★	★★★	★★★
With a 2	★★★★★	★★	★★★	★★★★	★
With a 3	★★	★★★	★★★★	★	★★★★
With a 4	★★★	★★★★	★	★★★★★	★★
With a 5	★★★	★	★★★★	★★	★★★
With a 6	★	★★★★	★★★★★	★★★	★★★★
With a 7	★★★★	★★★★★	★★★★	★★★★★	★
With an 8	★★★★	★★★★	★★★★★	★★	★★★★
With a 9	★★★★	★★★	★★★★	★★★★	★★★★
With an 11	★★★	★★★★★	★★	★★★★★	★★
With a 22	★★★	★★★	★★★★	★★	★★★

| 7 | 8 | 9 | 1 | 2 | 3 | 4 | 5 | 6 |

6	7	8	9	11	22
★	★★★★	★★★★	★★★★	★★★	★★★
★★★★	★★★★★	★★★★	★★★	★★★★★	★★★
★★★★★	★★★★	★★★★★	★★★★	★★	★★★★
★★★	★★★★★	★★	★★★★	★★★★★	★★
★★★★	★	★★★★	★★★★	★★	★★★
★★★★	★	★★★★	★★★★	★★★	★★★★★
★	★★★★	★★★	★★	★★★★★	★★★★★
★★★★	★★★	★★★★	★★★★	★★★★★	★★★
★★★★	★★	★★★★	★★	★★★★	★★★★
★★★	★★★★★	★★★★★	★★★★	★★★★★	★★★★
★★★★★	★★★★★	★★★	★★★★	★★★★	★★

6 5 4 3 2 1 9 8 7

Preferring friends whose minds are disciplined and educated, you nevertheless enjoy aspects of many different people socially. Let's see which are the best combinations ... and which are the worst:

7 and 1 (★★★★): You have similar needs and a wish to be afforded some privacy, yet you understand each other's mental and emotional state rather well. You may not admire **1**'s ego or their capacity to talk across others, but mostly this is a good friendship and you will tell them what's what – if anyone can!

7 and 2 (★★★★★): The gentle and passive nature of **2** makes a good friendship for a **7**, though you will some-times feel they are emotionally a little weak or clingy. **2**, in fact, deserves your admiration for their graceful personal style and good heart, and will look to you for excellent advice and sharp assessments. A good bond.

7 and **3** (★★★★): You two usually become good friends, with **3** verbalizing your observations with extra relish. Though you may have different ideas on choice of venue for a night out and your basic ethic for life, **3** makes you laugh and looks up to you as a wise companion.

7 and **4** (★★★★★): This is one of your best friends. **4** allows you that little precedence that you enjoy being given, yet pulls you gently back to earth if you get too nebulous in your ideas or with your emotions. Sometimes **4** seems a little tactless to you, but they are honest!

7 and **5** (★): Gunpowder and spark coming together! If you are lucky and have another number in common, you may live to enjoy the tensions, but overall a **5** will make you feel frantic and unrestful. You can only tolerate that boisterous exuberance for an hour or two – and don't let them start talking about their relationships ...

6 5 4 3 2 1 9 8 7

7 and **6** (★): A test of **6**'s generosity. **7** is a wise friend for many, but for a **6** you're on a different planet. You are provoked to be at your most caustic and intolerant with this sensualist, and they grow weary listening to your views, and become irritated by your food and health habits. Nor is **6**'s mind disciplined enough for you. Make a new friend!

7 and **7** (★★★★): It's possible that you will annoy each other, at least occasionally: you are just too alike and will each feel that you are right all the time. But you have a devastating shared sense of humour and very similar tastes. An 'all or nothing' witty, but knife-edge, bond!

7 and **8** (★★★): An **8** has a different set of values from you in some ways, but you enjoy their philosophical discussions and their explorations deep into the soul of humankind. **8** is also very generous, and helps you to laugh at yourself now and again. Friends!

7	8	9	1	2	3	4	5	6

7 and 9 (★★): More tricky. A **9** seems to lack focus and be too tied up with a vast array of friends. Their personal life seems convoluted – even messy – to you, and there may be too much exchange of truth here at times. **7** is honest but not necessarily brutal. What does **9** provoke you to say?

7 and 11 (★★★★★): Another good friendship – though do draw a line if **11** wallows a little too much sometimes. **11** feels life acutely, as do you; natural snobs, the pair of you (admit it!), **11** will adore your grace and poise, and you will love their charming never-say-die attitude.

7 and 22 (★★★★★): Someone you can respect will always be a friend. Here is such a person – intelligent and careful, determined, and possibly even fearless. A **22** friend will get you off your backside when you're in danger of shutting down from the world too much! Good for you.

6 5 4 3 2 1 9 8 7

7 IN OTHER PLACES

So what does it mean when your number turns up on a house? Do you live in a 7 home? And how does the number 7 affect your pet – or even the car that you drive? Numbers exude a subtle influence on everything in our lives; and here are just a few examples of how ...

A 7 address

If the number of your address – or of your apartment – reduces back to a 7, treat this dwelling as a haven of peace. A 7 home demands that you leave your dirty shoes and problems at the door, for here is an environment for meditation and thought, for clean habits and a positive lifestyle. The owners of a 7 house take pride in it, and live with dignity and good manners.

To fit in well with the nature of the home, whoever lives here must develop a good mind, self-reliance and a spirit of reverence for others. It will suit a writer, researcher or analyst very well – and if you are interested in growing herbs or learning about healing ways, put in an offer! If you're unprepared, or unwilling, to live alone sometimes, choose the house next door: 7 as the keynote for a home demands inner reflection and self-questioning, which cannot be done with too much noisy distraction.

6 5 4 3 2 1 9 8 7

A 7 pet

If you don't know your pet's birthday, use the first letter of their name to calculate their number. If it's a G, P or Y, they're a **7**. Whatever nature of pet this is, note its refined character! This animal prefers socializing with like-minded pets who are well-groomed and smell clean, and will ignore any snarling scrappers or mangy animals who try to get its attention. An animal of sophisticated tastes, and with a palate for a healthy diet, this creature will heal you quietly when you're feeling down – not that they jump all over you: a **7** asks you to approach the bench when you have something to ask. But such aristocratic behaviour makes it special when they gently come within stroking range.

Oh, and when your **7** pet is feeling a trifle irritated, watch out! No wheedling will entice them to let you mess with their plans. They may sit or lie at a distance, watching the horizon, thinking about the world as it goes by.

Make sure you give it regular walks (even a rabbit or a cat!), because this is where a **7** draws inspiration and unwinds from the stresses of life. Even a **7** pet.

A 7 car

If the numbers of your licence plate reduce to **7**, you must make the effort to get on with this vehicle. Sure to be a specialized car (with leather trim?) rather than the standard basic product, this is a machine with a mind. In fact, it may have so much intuition about speed cameras and road traps that it's worth letting it decide for you which route to take! A **7** car wants constant maintenance, and only the best accoutrements will do. The blanket in the back ought really to be cashmere, and please – no pink dice hanging from the rear-view mirror! Such an affront will force it to complain with frequent visits to the garage. Treat this car with respect, and it will grow old graciously!

YOUR LIFE NUMBER
Your lesson to learn

The time has come to consider the other main number in your numerology chart: your Life Lesson, or LIFE, number. This is sometimes also called the 'Birth Force'. Just as for the DAY number, calculating your LIFE number is easy: simply add together each digit of your full birth date (day, month and year), and keep adding the digits until they reduce to a single number (*see example on page 270*).

And that's it. You have your Life number.

So what does it tell us?

7   8   9   1   2   3   4   5   6

What does it mean?

The **LIFE** number takes times to show its mark. You should see its influence over many years, and understand that it is representative of certain strengths and weaknesses that we learn to live with through years of experience. These characteristics need to be analysed over time, and it can take a while for us to come to know ourselves truly from our **LIFE** number. Uncovering these aspects of our character is a process of discovery, and we often don't fully recognize the traits of this number as clearly, or as quickly, as those of the stronger **DAY** number.

Once you have done your sums and discovered this second important number, you'll want to find out what this means. If your **LIFE** and **DAY** numbers are the same, this powerfully reinforces the qualities of your own number, and accentuates both strengths and weaknesses. You won't be fighting corners within your personality by having two numbers to live with that are, perhaps, miles apart in spirit. But then, equally, if your numbers are the same you may lack a broad vision of the world, seeing with very sharp eyes through just a single (though enormous!) window.

On the following pages we will examine what your **DAY** number **7** is like in tandem with each other number, beginning with the powerful doubling of **7 DAY** and **7 LIFE**, and then moving on through all other possible combinations. If you discover you have a **LIFE** number which totals **11** or **22**, before it reduces to a final single digit of **2** or **4**, read the entry for **7** and **2**, or **7** and **4**, but also pay special attention to any extra information given relating to the added significance of the number being a variation of a master number.

SAME **DAY** AND **LIFE** NUMBER

With **7** as the predominant number in your life, your world is sure to be full of adventures with dolphins and salsa-dancing sessions. As an intense but essentially warm person, you tend to go into things with all of your energy, and are sure to be surrounded by people who are attracted to your zeal for life. With Michelangelo, Mozart and Almodóvar as your best friends, you are certain to entice and fascinate all around you. Yet, while the greats are often forgiving of our little vices, remember that this may not be so for the rest of the world: your tendency towards stubbornness or certainty can land you in trouble ...

6   5   4   3   2   1   9   8   7

Double trouble?

As a double **7**, you need to bear in mind that – with your innumerable talents – it never hurts to be a little more generous to others. Yes, maybe you're convinced that your way is the right way (and perhaps it is), but you should, nevertheless, always recognize others' efforts, even if they aren't up to your incredibly high standards.

Coleridge and Wordsworth had nothing on you: your intense powers of contemplation and self-sufficiency are enviable, leaving you chanting with the angels or seeing pure poetry in a violet. Your unique style and fashion sense mean that you often cut a swathe with your 1920s originals or your 1940s chic. But yet, your individual sense of timekeeping does not always mean that you make it to the ball before twelve: you are undoubtedly still thanking the pumpkin. Excellent at spotting talent across the dining table, you are sure to capitalize before anyone else does.

| 7 | 8 | 9 | 1 | 2 | 3 | 4 | 5 | 6 |

There is no question that the latest chef or the newest designer will be on your books, and you have just the bon mot to describe them.

Body and mind

Your need for cleanliness borders on the neurotic occasionally, and you may even have a clean mug in your handbag for visits to your mother – unless she, too, is a double **7**. Your body is not simply a temple – it's the Taj Mahal, and you are certainly one to respect it. But don't be afraid of modern innovations like the microwave – it's our friend! And, while your knowledge of the latest alternative remedies is second to none, be careful your breakfast table doesn't collapse under the weight of your wholegrain cereals and stewed prunes.

When this world is simply too tiresome, you are expert at disappearing into a good book. You will never waste your time on the bestseller chart, though, always preferring to obtain advanced proofs and read the newest Booker Prize winner even before they know they have been nominated!

With numerous contacts in your little black book, the notches on your bedpost would be the talk of a 'kiss and tell' for certain – but we can be sure that you never will. Not one for a simple 'tall, dark, and handsome', any partner of yours will have to move comfortably from tango shoes to hiking boots to climb the nearest hill or mountain. But beware those lovers that are not replete in themselves; you are not a nanny service, and the last thing a **7** wants is to babysit.

With your eye for design, your house will forever look like the domicile of a singleton, finished with beautifully scented flowers and high-end fireplaces (even if there's a toddler on the roam). With such a veracious mind, you are certain never to be bored, and you will keep your birds of a feather close to the nest. Endlessly entertaining to listen to, you are often happiest in your own company.

One of a kind

Known for your mannerisms and signature touches by all – that brooch or scarf, the way you tip your head or lick the plate(!), that small nod or downward look – no person will ever change you. Your friends know your mind as their personal research library, and any actual book they wish to borrow you probably have in your collection, too. Feisty in the bedroom, you're choosy but surprisingly libidinous, and poor fool the partner in your life who stops doing the washing-up or arrives at your healthily cooked dinner with dirty fingernails!

An interesting blend of rational thinking and spiritual awareness, critical appraisal of self and others and forgiving feelings towards those who interest you, you are enviably

6 5 4 3 2 1 9 8 7

happy with your own mind. Without compromising your search for truth and your wish to be free from delusion, if anyone could talk to an angel it most certainly would be you – although you probably won't believe anyone else who says they can!

DIFFERENT **DAY** AND **LIFE** NUMBERS

Most of us will find that we have two different birthday numbers, and this can be an advantage. One number may soften the single track of the other, and mean we can see other people's viewpoints more easily. At other times, though, the numbers may be in real conflict – and this leads to vacillation in our reactions to everyday situations, or confusion about why we want to run one way and then another.

In the following pages you will discover how your own two numbers are likely to work together, and what you can do to maximize the potential of both when they are paired up.

6   5   4   3   2   1   9   8   7

7 Day with 1 Life

This makes you competitive. You are clever, and you know it, but it is never enough to be just 'one of the clever ones'. You need to be at the top of your game all the time, and you will learn from your mistakes well. Your mind is finely disciplined and, though you are sensitive to others' criticisms of you, you are even more critical of yourself. You have a sharp analytical faculty married to a fast tongue, so journalism or writing will have an appeal for you. But heaven help those who annoy or hinder you, because you have a long memory and an utter dislike of fools.

This is a very private number-pairing. You really do need quiet time, and you will brood when feeling stressed or threatened. Circumstances will frequently foist private time upon you, and often you will deliberately push yourself out of your comfort zone just to challenge your mind and energies. Once the world around you becomes a known quantity, you will look to other stimuli to see how you fare, and at times this is both laudable and crazy! Something in you cannot settle, but setting yourself difficult objectives is part of what you're here for. Just don't be surprised if those who share your life become both confused and frustrated by this tendency.

You're not only original, but also a specialist. Nothing irks you more than dilettantism, and you will force yourself through some high hoops to learn everything there is to know about a subject. This makes you a first-class teacher, and many people who have these two numbers will be drawn by academic study and vocation. The solitude of research and writing up your findings will suit you too. On top of this, **7/1** is a bookish number-combination and, whatever genre you prefer, you will read a great deal. You also have a love of art and architecture, and an intellectual interest in metaphysical subjects.

6   5   4   3   2   1   9   8   7

With both of these numbers you may not have a large family, for the emphasis is on the intensity of personal bonds. Love will never be easy, either, for you ask a lot and you want to give particular aspects of yourself. Neither one of these numbers would settle for anything routine or humdrum, nor are they likely to have a conventional lifestyle. Put both together and you double the effect. You will alternately like (and need) both city and countryside, and you will definitely benefit from away-days which take you to the green world, or to the water. A vista of trees or the sea is part of what helps you to think philosophically, and such a sea- or landscape is bound to feature in the life you arrange.

7 Day with 2 Life

You may not, according to some of your friends, be altogether realistic about life, for the **7** will make you reach even higher than the **2** to the world of perfection and personal thought. 'Retreat', actually, in all of its meanings, is a good keyword for this pair of numbers. **7**s retreat from a world if things are less than they should be – if people don't strive enough for excellence and truth, or if situations are less vivid in reality than in the planning. **2** shares this idealism, and often shrinks, more than retreats, from those who let them down. But this is to emphasize only the troubled waters between these numbers, because the strengths that come with the **2** in your birthday are exceptional.

You will be high-minded and have an inherent nobility about you. Friends, loves and co-workers see you as apart from the dross, and understand that you are sensitive to injustices. You are a champion of the weak and the poor, and feel that the human race owes it to the planet always to behave like a gracious guest – though you are more than aware that this is rarely the case, and so you often feel let down by the true picture. But, with luck, you never quite give up hope that something can be done to make things better. Refined, deep-thinking, spiritual and philosophical, your two numbers ask that you lead a life of service to others, and that responsibilities sit with you over many years. And you give all of this without too much complaint.

The number **7** sharpens the perceptions of the number **2**, so that you become a specialist. **7** combats **2**'s indecisiveness, and you will go out on a limb to learn everything you can about a subject. You move from teacher to professor, doctor to consultant, musician to soloist, and need to discover the best skills you have and be at the top of your game. Writing may be a considerable talent for you, too.

7   8   9   1   2   3   4   5   6

2 loves its family, but **7** often enforces the need of some solitude, so you may have a smaller family or find a way to live both with and away from those you love. This time is needed for your mind to dwell on what is important. Neither **2** nor **7** is a selfish number, so you will possibly feel tugged to perform many acts of kindness or charity for others, or simply to work in a selfless field. Research is likely to be at least a part of what you do. And, with these two numbers working with you, your life will be lived at a high level of professionalism in everything you do. Make sure you have trees, or a view of the sea, to counter the stress you put yourself under.

7 Day with 3 Life

A **DAY** number of 7 adds some healthy sobriety to exuberant 3, and makes you discerning and self-critical, though still very artistic and appreciative of people. Kind-hearted and a good judge of character, you will nevertheless withdraw into your shell more often than a **DAY 3** would. A relationship which gives you breathing space and time by yourself is a virtual must. Your taste is impeccable – the 7 accentuating this quality in 3 – and your memory rapier-sharp, though selective. You hang on to a kind deed or a cruel hurt in equal measure.

7 is the number of truth and, as 3 urges you to speak, you will have much of value to say. It is unusual for you to take anything at face value because you size up situations astutely, but your **LIFE** number 3 helps you to grow into such easy charm that others may be unaware that they

are being analysed. The numbers together give you powerful intuitive skills, and it is hard to imagine anyone pulling the wool over your eyes.

However, you can be surprisingly idealistic, and invest great expectation in those you love. A refined sensibility leads you to hope that everyone else will behave with moral goodness, and it will hurt when they inevitably let you down. Coping with these punches is something you will do after many years of gradually hardening yourself to some of life's realities.

But the entertainment committee that is **3** does not desert you just because of the daily presence of serious-thinking **7**. You plan out – and execute – star-studded events with exactitude. Full of resources, you know exactly where to find a stork ice sculpture for the baby shower, or a unicorn piñata for the church fete. You can find ice cream in the Amazon and a taxi at midnight on New Year's Eve; and if anyone can charm the parking attendant out of issuing a ticket on Fifth Avenue, it will be you! The irresistible blend of **7**'s inner serenity and elegance with the charm and natural flirtatiousness of **3** is at its peak in this number-pairing.

You should work for yourself, for you are all things to all people. Independent as well as sociable, focused as well as multi-faceted, you manage to see a dozen tasks to their conclusion all at once. Like a Bach fugue, you have many themes working together with great complexity ... and such is the complexity of character you are: lightness with gravity, friendliness with reticence. Allow yourself the scope to respond to circumstances in different ways on different days. And don't be worried if you constantly surprise even yourself.

7 Day with 4 Life

All of the overlap between these two numbers emerges like crystal, when someone has this **DAY/LIFE** combination. **7**'s nobler spirit directs **4**'s tireless energy daily, to splendid effect. **7** prefers never to dirty its fine, surgical hands – but this is not a squeamishness that **4** suffers from, and as a result the finely architected notions born in **7**'s imagination can take real physical shape sculpted by **4**'s deft hands. And again, **7** operates from a more informed understanding of people's feelings, and thereby mellows **4**'s honest tongue, making it less biting or unintentionally cruel.

These two numbers agree on points of hygiene and cleanliness, so a **7/4** with a dirty hairbrush or an old or worn-out bathroom simply cannot be imagined! The bathroom may be the most important room in your house, and, along with clean bedlinen and a neatly organized office space, money spent on bedroom and bathroom would be an absolute priority. The 7 also heightens the 4's ability to concentrate and dwell deeply on a problem, so long nights of music and chess games, or many hours spent walking in the country, will produce interesting, analytical results.

When it comes to friends, you may have only a few, but they will be loyal and true, and 'birds of a feather'. And a lover will have had to face the most stringent tests of moral character and intellectual soundness just to be with you. But lest we make you sound too worthy, 7's humour married to 4's love of the practical joke makes you superb company for the discerning mind.

And 4's well-publicized DIY skills could certainly be put to good use building bookshelves: these numbers put together will read their way through pretty much everything in the local library. And do you write? The combination of these two numbers gives you not only a capacity for analysis and word play, but also the self-reliance to go away quietly, sit down, and do it. You are likely to specialize in factual work.

| 6 | 5 | 4 | 3 | 2 | 1 | 9 | 8 | 7 |

7 Day with 5 Life

A lethal mix of quick wit and sharp tongue can occasionally make **7** an unpopular number, but here LIFE number **5** spares **7** the criticism of others, and instead the qualities of both numbers combine to produce a developed and entertaining raconteur. The sociable, party-loving **5** lightens **7**'s sometimes over-analytical personality, making you a must for every dinner party and cocktail do in town. **7**'s shrewd intelligence sometimes puts **5**'s creativity on a back-burner, but the two together make you an acute critic and a great admirer of art, literature and music.

DAY 7 directs LIFE 5 to far more focus than you would otherwise expect from such a restless number, and others may find the intensity with which you do things both terrifying and enticing. **5** does everything, knows everyone and is seen everywhere, and typically has fantastic creative

| 7 | 8 | 9 | 1 | 2 | 3 | 4 | 5 | 6 |

ideas and is then bored of them by the time the next course has arrived. **7**'s enviable determination utilizes **5**'s ability to do so many different things, and channels **5**'s often excessive energy towards truly useful projects, rather than seeing it dissipated. **7** is a very private number, often mulling over decisions for many days, while **5** is more of an extrovert. **5**'s often surprising stubbornness fuels **7**'s inclination to brood, and it is not uncommon for **5** to furiously voice the comments that **7** might ordinarily keep under wraps – but with such humour!

7 provides **5** with the drive to succeed at one thing until it is done: **7** detests dilettantism, and instead forces your often unruly **5** side to direct itself towards reaching the very highest levels of its potential. **5**'s passionate and sexy personality combined with **7**'s frighteningly high standards means that serious love relationships will not always be easily found, but fervent office affairs make you a vixen or a sex god not to be trifled with. Your reputation is one of envied ruthlessness – 7's intolerant nature roused by 5's surplus energy – making you both a feared opponent and a revered colleague.

Often the 7/5 combination channels 5's creativity into 7's serious talent for writing and analysis, and back again through 5's gift of the gab. An eye for aesthetics means that your house is perfectly laid out and designed. Yet, sometimes 7 can be too clinical, overshadowing 5's freer personality; be sure to let all of your 5 warmth out as the years pass, and don't *always* be ruled by more serious 7. It is sometimes hard for people to get close to you – given the high standards you set for those around you – but knowing you well is both an education and a privilege.

7   8   9   1   2   3   4   5   6

7 Day with 6 Life

There's serious taste and style here! This is an explosive combination of numbers, with **7**'s quick wit and sharp tongue giving **6**'s enviable people skills the forum to be displayed at their best. You are a raconteur par excellence, and everyone wants to be near you. There is a charm and sparkle about **7** which your **6 LIFE** number makes more accessible — softening the bite! — and, with invitations to your best friend's birthday and the Black and White Ball alike, you are sure to delight all with your humour and charisma. There is a magic about **7** that makes it an alluring and yet frightening number to be around. It is not uncommon for people to take offence at **7**'s wittily cutting remarks, but here **6** saves the day, with its masterful people skills and basic kindness, ensuring that everyone can laugh at themselves.

| 6 | 5 | 4 | 3 | 2 | 1 | 9 | 8 | 7 |

7 adds grit to **6**'s natural aptitude for so many things, and this combination of numbers is not uncommon in managing directors, politicians and chairpeople. A **6** might be better at making something out of other people's creative works rather than their own, but the **7 DAY** number lends a steely business sense to **6**'s eye for beauty. It really is a powerful pairing of numbers, with **6**'s persuasive talents (watch them sell a signed Mick Jagger picture to a Beatles fan using gentle charm!) and **7**'s killer instinct when it comes to business. You are destined to be modelling the latest trends in the newest sports car, the next time you pull up at the tennis club. **6** by no means lacks ambition, but **7** provides the necessary nous to drive home the advantage where **6** might otherwise shy away.

Though each can be surprisingly retiring at times, **6** added to **7** bestows the confidence to carry off those skyscraper heels without flinching, and to approach the sexy Martini-quaffer in the bar with effortless grace. But **6** also mellows the often quirky **7**'s need for a challenge — perhaps making you content just to have a quiet drink with rallying friends, instead of running off to the club to publicly admonish a faithless lover or a disappointing business associate. **7** gives **6** that necessary lift which makes you a bee with a killer sting. **6** may hold their tongue in public, but with a **7 DAY** number, you certainly never will!

There is no question that a **7/6** combination is not to be trifled with. Your stellar instincts make you queen of the office or king of the cartel, while your smooth moves and easy manner ensure you are surrounded by people. Take advantage of your natural attributes and work your **7**'s sharpness. You have **6**'s sweetness to convince the traffic warden you really didn't realize loading bays were for industrial deliveries, and not just for quick purchases at Manolo Blahnik.

7 Day with 8 Life

This is an intellectual and reflective pair of numbers. **8** can dominate other numbers with its sheer veracity and force of will, but **DAY 7** directs its noble intentions, showing **8** how to blend in, with more refined manners and greater tact. **8** is sensitive of others' feelings, and **7** is aware of what is below the surface: together these numbers give you X-ray vision and an uncanny sense of what is developing. **8** is also a very godly number – in a rather ecumenical sense – and **7**'s spirituality directing this energy can lead to some astonishing realizations and understanding. Anyone with birthday numbers of **7** and **8** together will prompt friends and family to personal epiphanies at 'crossroads' moments.

The bad news is that your lack of tolerance for foolish minds and shallow thinkers just doubled! **8** only associates

7   8   9   1   2   3   4   5   6

with inquisitive and disciplined minds, so add this to 7's dignity and you've got a problem coping with banality. However, even in a room full of humourless automatons, having these numbers inherent in your mindset helps you float to the clouds and come back with some material advantage. And it is good for 7 — often a little unaware of the need to live in a material world — to have the more practical and financially minded 8 backing it up. 8 really does like to earn money — not least because it is hugely generous, and likes the freedom to roam mentally that money enables. 7 doesn't mean to be cautious about funds, but often doesn't have that freedom to act spontaneously because money has not been a priority.

On the skill front, 7 partnering 8 brings serious musical ability and interest — and also, perhaps, a love of, or aptitude for, sports. 8 has sheer talent and rhythm — being the number of the octave; 7 adds that concentrated awareness that hard work is required if a talent is to be more than just that. **7/8** needs a good and extended education to support the intellectual wanderings it wishes to make. And you will very much need to be loved, because **8** is a harmonic number, adding a chorus behind **7**'s solo virtuosity.

Despite **8**'s unquestionable charm, it often lacks self-discipline, but **7** guides this. **8**, once it has tasted success, has amazing powers of organization at home, and also outside in the wider world. **7**'s analytical strengths blend well with **8**'s good judgement to produce a fine mind with an old soul, and someone who – although you like people – will never be truly at home with the common crowd. Though **7** is not always adaptable, **8**'s talents married to **7** give you authority and recognition, allowing you perhaps to find that judicious balance between the more public and the more private sides of your nature.

7 Day with 9 Life

The number **9** colours **7**'s artistry with dramatic flavours and textures. **7** looks beneath the surface to know what another person is thinking; **9** feels as they are feeling. Given the blend of these two numbers, then, drama and writing are possible vocations for a **7/9** to take. What is interesting, though, is that this combination intensifies the idealism inherent in both numbers, so the presence of **9** makes the most romantic version of **7** imaginable. **7**'s dignity and elegance also vivifies **9**'s already considerable personal magnetism, so we are looking at quite an impressive teaming of numbers.

With **9** urging you to get on with a broader group of friends, **7**'s antithesis to larger gatherings is somewhat smoothed over: **9** helps **7** overcome what is a mixture of shyness and pride to let its real inner warmth be felt by others. That number **9** also makes a huge impact on the level of your physical energy, enticing you to get out and join in life at the actual rather than the cerebral level. **7** is sometimes very reserved, but **9** is gregarious and sociable. This makes the **7** humour more palatable and, though your critical element never leaves you behind, whatever you say probably comes out with a blend of archness and sweetness that makes it impossible for anyone to take offence. **9** is also very responsible, and this, too, steers **7** away from that tendency to stay out of other people's affairs because it seems ill-mannered to intrude. With **9** and **7** together, you will often intrude – and will be heartily thanked for it.

In women, **9** makes more of a sexy lioness out of discerning **7**. You will leave that distinctive lipstick mark on your wine glass, which fills in a hundred unspoken words to the lover you are quarrelling with. The parting jibe is unnecessary, as **9** has dramatic flair and **7** the cool authority to leave the room in total control. And the next day you'll be bombarded with messages and apologies – and *you* will decide when to answer them. This is because 9's sense of the broader picture helps 7 get out of that hurt place where it might otherwise just retire to lick its wounds.

One interesting manifestation of 7 and 9 within one individual is that, for all that beauty and nobility of character, there is a disconcerting lack of certainty in what you do. You may be timid when others least expect it from you, or you may vacillate and become moody, and refuse to clinch an option or an opportunity. At times, these delays are very costly. Just remember that your numbers married together blend exceptional style and taste with a deep feeling for how to turn unlovely things into lovelier ones. Believe in yourself more, for there's no doubt that everyone else does!

6 5 4 3 2 1 9 8 7

THE FUTURE
Take a look what's in store...

And now we come to the calculation of your future.
Each year, on your birthday, you move into a new
sphere of number-influence which governs that year.
The numbers progress in cycles of nine years; after
nine years, the cycle starts over again, and a whole
new period of your life begins afresh. The cycle can
be applied to every number, so you can discover what
the main issues will be for partners, friends and
family, as well as for yourself, in any given year (*see
calculation instructions, opposite*). Emphasis is placed
on what will happen to you when you are in your
own year number – that is, in any '7' year cycle.

| 7 | 8 | 9 | 1 | 2 | 3 | 4 | 5 | 6 |

Working out your cycle

To find out what year you're currently in, use the same formula employed for calculating the **LIFE** number, but substitute the current year for the year in which you were born. Every year, the cycle then moves on by one more number until, after a **9** year, returning to **1**, to begin the cycle again.

Calculation example 1

BIRTHDAY: 25 July 1982

TO CALCULATE THE CURRENT YEAR NUMBER: $2+5+7+\left[\underset{\text{CURRENT YEAR}}{2+0+0+7}\right] = 23$, and $2+3 = $ **5**

*This means that on 25 July 2007 you move into a **5** year. On 25 July the following year, this would then move into a **6** year (2+5+7+2+0+0+8 = 24, and 2+4 = **6**), and the year after that, a **7** year, and so on.*

6	5	4	3	2	1	9	8	7

Calculation example 2

BIRTHDAY: 16 December 1963

TO CALCULATE THE $1+6+1+2+\begin{bmatrix} 2+0+0+7 \\ \text{CURRENT YEAR} \end{bmatrix}=19/1+9 = 10$
CURRENT YEAR NUMBER: and $1+0 = \mathbf{1}$

This means that on 16 December 2007 you move into a **1** *year. On 16 December the following year, this would then move into a* **2** *year (1+6+1+2+2+0+0+8 = 20, and 2+0 =* **2**), *and the year after that, a* **3** *year, and so on.*

Many numerologists feel that the impact of a year number can be felt from the first day of that year – in other words, from 1st January. However, the usual school of thought is that the new number cycle is initiated *on your birthday itself*, and my experience tends to corroborate this. So, if your birthday is fairly late in the year – November or December, say – this means that you will have gone through most of the calendrical year before *your* new number-year cycle for that year begins.

Look back over some recent years, and see if – in the descriptions on the following pages – you can pinpoint the moment when your yearly number-cycle for any given year became apparent. You'll be amazed at just how accurate this system seems to be.

A 1 year

This is the perfect time to set up new and quite specific long-term goals, and consider just where you want to be a few years from now. You will have new people around you from this point on, and fresh ideas about them and the interests they awaken in you. This is a completely new chapter in your life, and you should set goals for a better and more fulfilling future.

Career-wise, a **1** year often occurs at a time of new employment, or of a complete change in direction in your working life. You are probably wanting to develop new skills or make use of untested talents. You have to believe in yourself now. This is the time when it's a little easier to step back and see how to get started along a particular path. Goals, you will understand, are perfectly attainable, even if a year ago they seemed unrealistic. In a **1** year you have tremendous focus and independence, and excellent determination.

The secret to your success now is in your ability to concentrate; but, emotionally, things can be quite testing. No matter how strong a love bond may be in your life, a **1** year demands that you do much for yourself. You could feel isolated or unsupported, even if someone dear is close by. This is a test of your own courage and inner strength. Only your strongest desires will gain results ... but then, your desires should be fierce during this cycle. Try not to act impulsively, as the push to do so will be powerful, but also, don't be afraid to be independent and go your own way. Strong urges are driving you – forward, for the most part – and a **1** year lends you exceptional clarity and energy.

A 2 year

A year which demands co-operation and partnerships at every level, **2** is a gentle year cycle, when you can consolidate what you started in the previous twelve months. You will need to be diplomatic and sensitive towards other people's feelings, but your intuition is very strong now, and you are able to share the load and the initiative more than you were allowed last year. For this reason, don't try to push things too far or too fast. After the previous whirlwind year, this is a moment to take your time and get things right.

Relationships come more into focus during a **2** year. This is especially pleasing if someone new entered your life in the last year or so, for the vibration of **2** helps a bond to strengthen, and a feeling of mutuality improves now. In some ways you may feel the desire or the need to be secretive, but this is because there are unknown elements at work all on fronts. It will affect you at work and at play, and in a close tie you will discover new tenderness that will probably separate you from other friends. If there is no one special currently in your life, this may be the year to find someone: a **2** year brings a relationship much stronger than a fling!

Your negotiation skills and ability to guess what another person is feeling may work very well for you this year; and, if the number **2** derives from master number **11** (which it almost surely will), there is a chance for serious partnerships and master opportunities. You will need to look at contracts carefully, and spend time on legalities. But this is often the most exciting and unusual year out of the nine. Mysteries come to light, and your ideas flow well. Just be prepared to consider another person in every equation.

A 3 year

Time for you! This twelve-month period is concerned with developing your abilities and testing your flexibility. Your imagination is especially strong, and you may have particular opportunities to improve your wealth and make lasting friendships. You will also need to be focused, because the energy of a **3** year is fast and furious, and may make you feel dissolute. Usually, though, this is a happy year spent with some travel prospects and many creative inspirations. Difficulties which intruded in the previous two years are often resolved in this year cycle.

Business and your social life often run together in a **3** year, and work will be a lot of fun. It is worth taking time over your appearance and indulging yourself more than usual, for the sociability of this number brings you many invitations and a chance to create a new look, or to explore

7   8   9   1   2   3   4   5   6

other aspects of your personality. You have extra charm this year, so try to use it where it is needed.

Many people find that the number **3** expresses itself in a year cycle as a third person to consider: frequently, this is the birth of a child or an addition to the family, but it might be that another party pressures you in your personal relationship. Don't talk too much about this, or show nervousness. Under a **3** vibration, it is easy to become exhausted — even through over-excitement — so be alert to the impulse towards extravagance and fragmentation. Try to enjoy the way in which you are being drawn out of yourself this year, and allow yourself time to study, write, paint. Anything you really want you can achieve now — even strange wishes and desires can be pulled towards you. Make sure you think a little about what you are asking for!

6   5   4   3   2   1   9   8   7

A 4 year

A much-needed year of good-housekeeping – on the personal level, as well as literally. This year will demand practicality from you. Often a **4** brings a focus on money or accounts, on repairs around the home, or on putting your life into better order. It may not be what you want, yet it will force itself upon you. It is sometimes a year spent with a pen in hand – writing lists or cheques, doing sums and keeping diaries. It is also a year when you will need to do some research, to find out about what you don't know.

You have so much work to do in a **4**, or **22**, year – more than for a long time. Your personal pleasure takes second place to requirement, and it may seem difficult to stick to the task sometimes. Money demands that you do so, for extra expenditure is not advised in this twelve-month period. Yet if this sounds stressful, it also gives you a feeling of satisfaction that you will achieve so much this year – a job of hard work and dedication really well done. It may be that this year gives you a very good foundation for the future and sets up lasting improvements.

You will never survive a **4** – or, especially, a **22** – year if you are not organized and implement a system of work and life. Be honest in what you do with others, but also in what you do for yourself. You cannot deceive yourself, and must check details carefully. You may have a feeling of burden at times, but there is a chance to feel you have done something extraordinary, too. Translate your clever ideas into practical results. The most significant thing for you to do is to concentrate on proper personal management. The weight of the world is on your shoulders, but you can bear it if the preparations you make are good. There is no escape from demands on your time and intelligence, but nothing can be hurried, so face the job ahead and you will soon find you have climbed a hill to new vistas.

6 5 4 3 2 1 9 8 7

A 5 year

After careful management of your time last year, and a feeling of being tied to the wheel, this will seem like bursting from the inside of a darkened room into bright light. Now you have a change from routine to madness, and you may feel a personal freedom that was denied you last year. Nevertheless, nothing is completely settled in a **5** year, and this uncertainty may take its toll. Try to look at this cycle as a chance to find success in newer areas, and a way to advance from necessary stagnation into running waters of energy and vitality. You will update your sense of yourself during this period, and make progress towards the life you want, following the previous year's required self-discipline.

You are admitting to the need for new pastures, so your ideas of what your life might include, or who may have a role in it, may alter now. No one likes to be held back in a **5** year, but it is still important not to be too hasty in your actions. Use your energies, by all means, but govern them with your head. This is the time for innovation, and new takes on old goals, but if you quarrel with those dear to you, or with whom you work, it may be difficult to repair later. If change is still inevitable, be as kind and constructive as possible, and make sure you aren't leaping from one difficult situation straight into another. You need to discover your versatility and personal resourcefulness to get the best out of this cycle. And, for some of the twelve months, travel or lots of movement seems inescapable.

This year is potentially some kind of turning point for you. Learning how to adapt to sudden circumstances is vital, because any plans or directives set in stone will cause you pain, and possibly come unstuck. Be prepared for changes and, if this brings a nervousness with it, try to meet the adventure head-on. If you talk yourself up and take on a front-running position, you can work wonders in a **5** year.

A 6 year

Love is in the air. Other things seize your time too – your home needs attention, and duties demand your energy – but, principally, this year is about emotions and relationships. Sometimes love and happiness are a reward for surviving so much in the past two years, and for unselfish service and support for others. The emphasis is on finding harmony with others, and this may come in various ways. This year, you may have the impetus and opportunity to erase problems that have previously beset you. You understand, and feel acutely sensitive towards, others, and are more radiant and beautiful than you have been for some time. If you can be kind and positive in emotional dealings, you will benefit in many ways, including materially.

There are hurdles in a **6** year in connection with obligations you feel towards others. At times you are stretched,

7 8 9 1 2 3 4 5 6

because there are personal desires and ties you want to nurture which are countermanded by the duties you are subjected to. You may resent this, yet, if you can remain cheerful, you will be rewarded in ways not immediately apparent. Love is trying to sweep you off your feet, but your health may suffer because you are trying to fit in so much, and the intensity of your feelings is strong.

While it's good to be helpful in a **6** year, don't allow yourself to be taken advantage of, or let people drain you completely. Set up a system that lets you delegate some responsibility. Your home may bloom while you're in such a happy mood, and you should feel creative and mellow. The events of a **6** year are not as fast and furious as the previous year, but things move steadily towards a happier state of being. Let the time go as it will, because this is not a year to fight against what comes to you; get into the right philosophical gear and open yourself to pleasant surprises that come from being useful, and being warm with others.

A 7 year

This year is a time for manifesting your own most important goals by visualizing them. See yourself triumphing and continuing toward your vision. Never lose sight of what you want, or confusion will reign. You'll be tempted this way and that, annoyed by gossip, and attacked by those who love you but don't understand what you are trying to do. Don't be swayed by them, or you will lose your opportunities and precious time.

Keep your head, as everything depends on your state of mind. Refuse to react to distractions, and avoid hasty actions or sudden decisions. A calm approach is the best remedy to the chaos surrounding you. You may have to move house without warning, but take it in your stride and make a calm, clear choice on where to go. If you are travelling somewhere exotic, be prepared with vitamins

7   8   9   1   2   3   4   5   6

and medicines to avoid viruses of any kind.

Legal matters may arise during this year, relating to business, investments or house options. Consult an expert to avoid pitfalls, and, when you feel happy, proceed with confidence. If you have taken all the facts and details into account, you'll now be within sight of your goal. But watch your health, as the number 7 is connected with this subject for both good and ill. You might get fit and lose some weight or, conversely, suffer with some little grievance. This is a time for mental, spiritual and physical detoxing. Also, rest: take a vacation to the country, to a quiet location where you can think in peace. Let no one confuse you. You may have to wait, but you will know how to come out on top if you listen to your intuition.

This is an excellent year for you as a 7 – for study, research, writing and reading, and clearing out all the unnecessary people or ideas from your past.

6 5 4 3 2 1 9 8 7

An 8 year

This cycle brings the possible finding of a soulmate. If you're single, you could not have a better chance of meeting that special someone than now. **8** years also relate to money, so you may be caught up with an impossible workload and regard the arrival of such a potentially strong love as poor timing – and perhaps this is why it comes to you, because your attention being taken up elsewhere may be the best reason for someone's admiration. The love vibration you experience under karmic year number **8** may point to a future relationship prospect which has a lasting importance.

For those in settled relationships, pregnancy sometimes comes with this number, and it brings a very special link between the child and their parents. Or, you may experience a deep urge to study a subject that comes easily to you, though you have never learned about it before – a

7   8   9   1   2   3   4   5   6

language, perhaps, or an artistic skill you were attracted to but never developed, but which you now pick up well. Even a professional subject that you seem to grasp quickly will seem more important to perfect than ever before. Partly, this is because **8** year cycles concern making more money, and dealing with the deeply felt past. There are huge opportunities for you in an **8** year, and you will want to be prepared to maximize them. However, you'll need to use good judgement and be efficient with your time management.

Many people feel pushed to the limit in an **8** year, because there is just so much going on. Consider, though, that the vibration of the number wants to find positive expression, so the more efficiency and determination you can bring to it, the better the chance of finishing on a high note. Don't over-commit your time or money, and be ready to acquiesce to others' ways of doing things. You need to be confident, but ready to adjust too. **8** is made up of two circles, asking 'infinity' of you. But this year, you can do it!

A 9 year

Your personal affairs all come to a head in a **9** year, and whatever has been insufficient, or unsatisfying, will rise to the surface and demand change now. It could be the fulfilment of many dreams, for this is the culmination of nine years' experience. Whatever is jettisoned was probably no longer of use – though this might seem dispassionate. Many friendships will drift away, but you have probably outgrown them. The strongest demand of you is a readiness to discard what will not be part of your serious future – and this can mean a temporary feeling of insecurity.

You will certainly travel in a **9** year. Even if a trip is short, or of no great distance, it will settle something in your mind. The more compassionate, tolerant and forgiving you are, the more warmth and generosity will come to you. This is not the right moment to start something completely new, but if events arise as a natural conclusion to what has gone before, this is a good thing. Your mind needs to engage with bigger issues, for selfishness or petty ideas will cause you unhappiness under this number. People will thwart you in your career and personal matters – and these obstacles seem to come out of the blue, and are beyond your control. However, if you think on philosophical issues and remain open to big ideas, everything will turn out well.

A **9** year can be populated with many friends and activities, yet can feel lonely too; this is a cycle for completion of tasks and the ending of what is not enduring. But this is the right time to see the fruits of your previous work. Be wise about where your destiny seems to want to take you. Your artistic and imaginative facilities are inspired now, and you'll begin to see new directions that you know you must investigate in the years ahead. You know what is missing in your life, or where you've failed yourself, and can now prepare for the new adventure that's about to dawn.

6   5   4   3   2   1   9   8   7

How to find your DAY NUMBER

Add the digits for the day of birth, and keep adding them until they reduce to one number:

EXAMPLES

25 July 1982	2+5 = **7**
16 December 1963	1+6 = **7**

How to find your LIFE NUMBER

Add the digits for the day, month and year of birth, and keep adding them until they reduce to one number:

EXAMPLES

25 July 1982   2+5+7+1+9+8+2 = 34
and 3+4 = **7**

16 December 1963   1+6+1+2+1+9+6+3 = 29
2+9 = 11 (a 'master' number), and 1+1 = **2**

Further reading

The Complete Book of Numerology, David A. Phillips, Hay House, 2006

The Day You Were Born: A Journey to Wholeness Through Astrology and Numerology, Linda Joyce, Citadel Press, 2003

Many Things on Numerology, Juno Jordan, De Vorss Books, 1981

Numerology, Hans Decoz and Tom Monte, Perigee Books, 2001

Numerology: The Romance in Your Name, Juno Jordan, De Vorss Books, 1977

Sacred Number, Miranda Lundy, Wooden Books, 2006

The Secret Science of Numerology: The Hidden Meaning of Numbers and Letters, Shirley Blackwell Lawrence, New Page Books, 2001

About the author

Titania Hardie is Britain's favourite 'Good Witch' and a best-selling author. Born in Sydney, Australia, Titania has a degree in English and Psychology, and also trained in parapsychology and horary astrology. With a high media profile, she regularly appears on television in the UK, US, Canada, Australia and South Africa, as well as receiving widespread newspaper and magazine coverage. Her previous titles have sold over a million copies worldwide, and include Titania's Crystal Ball, Aroma Magic, and Hocus Pocus. Her first novel is due to be published in summer 2007.

Acknowledgements

Many thanks to you, Nick, for the clear and brilliant vision; you knew what you wanted and, like a true and inspired **1**, kept mulling it over until a way was found. This is your baby. Also big thanks to Tessa, master number **22**, for your commitment to this magnum opus beyond call: only you and I know, Tessa, how much time and soul has gone into all of these words. To Ian, for keeping us piping along with a true **4**'s sanguine approach to such a long body of work, and to Elaine and Malcolm for the look – **6**s, naturally! For my daughter Samantha, thanks for some of your ideas which found expression in the second-to-last section: I love the latte in Soho while signing the author. Let's see! To Georgia, for work in the field on number **5**, my thanks. To all of you, my appreciation, and I wish you all LUCKY NUMBERS!

EDDISON·SADD EDITIONS

Editorial Director **Ian Jackson**   Art Director **Elaine Partington**
Managing Editor **Tessa Monina**   Mac Designer **Karen Watts**
Proofreader **Nikky Twyman**   Production **Sarah Rooney**